SPAIN

The Best Places to See by Rail

An Alternative to the Escorted Tour

BOB KAUFMAN

**The Gelato Press
916 Pleasant Street
Norwood, MA 02062 USA**

SPAIN.. The Best Places to See by Rail An Alternative to the Escorted Tour

Copyright, 2021, by Bob Kaufman and The Gelato Press of Norwood, Massachusetts, USA

All rights reserved, printed in the United States of America. Absolutely no part of this book may be reproduced, distributed, or transmitted in any form or by any means, including photocopying, recording, or other electronic method without the prior written permission of the publisher, except in the case of brief quotations embodied in critical reviews and certain other non-commercial uses permitted by copyright law.

The information included in this book is believed to be correct at the time of publication. However, the reader should be cautioned to verify all routes and rates stated by the author with known websites on the internet. Train times stated, and travel times are approximate. Hotel and attraction rates are approximate. Please consult their websites for current information. The Euro vs. the US dollar used in this book is approximately $1.22-1.25 to purchase one Euro.

COVER PHOTO:
A Spanish Renfe AVE (Alta Velocidad Española) train reaches almost 200 MPH against a blazing sunset en route to Seville, passing the medieval Castle at Almodovar del Rio 25 miles south of Cordoba. Photo provided and used by permission of Renfe, the operator of the largest high-speed rail system in Spain and the second largest in the world. Photo by W. Patier.

BACK COVER
Back cover photos of the Bilbao Guggenheim Museum; the cellar at Casa Botin, Madrid; and the La Boqueria Market on the Ramblas in Barcelona, courtesy of the author and Lenore Brownstein.

The author can be reached at
thegelatopress@gmail.com
-or-
Bob Kaufman
The Gelato Press
916 Pleasant St #9
Norwood, MA, 02062 USA

ISBN-13: 979-8684495076

Other books by Bob Kaufman:

ITALY The Best Places to See by Rail
An Alternative to the Escorted Tour
ISBN-13: 9781985276802

ITALY Skip the Hotel and Stay at a Palace,
For the Same Price Live Like Royalty
ISBN-13: 9781792795626

ITALY Over 300 Critical Tips You Need to Know
Before You Go
ISBN-13: 9781677189281

Acknowledgments:

Lenore Brownstein, for being sequestered with me for four months while I wrote this book; Ella Kaufman for choosing the sub-title "*The Best Places to See by Rail*"; Linda and Emilio Sanvicente for providing the Spanish and Catalan translations; Suzzette Freedlander of the DSPOT for her cover design and book layout; Suzanne Slavitter and Daniel Chavez for debriefing me on their most recent visit to Spain; and Michelle Delacourt for her help with WORD and Adobe layouts.

Reviews on the back cover

DEDICATION

This book is dedicated to the 130 Spanish soles and 60 foreigners who perished on the morning of March 11, 2004, when four Madrid bound commuter trains were blown up by terrorists. Known as "11M," it was the second deadliest Al-Qaeda terrorist attack in Europe since Pan Am Flight 103 was blown up over Lockerbie, Scotland

MEET THE AUTHOR

Bob Kaufman has a passion for travel in Italy and Spain. He wrote his first book in June of 1983 about telecommunications. Although discontinued, it's still available on Amazon. After authoring three books on Italy he thought he would write his fifth book on Spain since few know there is an alternative to the expensive escorted tour. Bob has lots of experience on this subject. He ran those expensive tours! He is the past President of National Travel Vacations, Inc. (NTV) and for over 30 years specialized in group only tours on contract to travel agents in the USA.

Bob's an Eagle Scout, and when he is not digging clams in the summer on Cape Cod, he is enjoying the beautiful American Southwest in the winter with his travelling companion and partner Lenore. Bob and Lenore love Spanish food and of course gelato.

TABLE OF CONTENTS

INTRODUCTION 1
- **1** Spain, Spain, Spain…It's a Sleeper **14**
- **2** Four ways to visit Spain **22**
- **3** Critical things to do before we go **35**
- **4** First let's get to Spain **39**
- **5** Rail Itineraries Overview **53**
- **6** Barcelona and Madrid in Nine Days **62**
- **7** Barcelona Day Trips- Montserrat and Girona **104**
- **8** Madrid Day Trips- Toledo, Avila, El Escorial and Segovia **118**
- **9** Andalusia – Cordoba, Granada, Seville **143**
- **10** Malaga- Marbella and the Costa del Sol **170**
- **11** Seville and Costa del Sol Day Trips- Gibraltar, Ronda and Tangier Morocco **182**
- **12** The North: San Sebastian, Bilbao and the Santiago d Compostela **203**
- **13** The XYZ Tour **218**
- **14** Lisbon .. Yes it's Portugal **221**
- **15** The French Connection- RENFE-SNCF **226**
- **16** The Spain Eurail pass and other discounts **230**
- **17** Security, Money, Credit Cards, Telephones **239**
- APPENDIX **264**
- MAPS **268**

SPAIN
RAIL ITINERARIES

BARCELONA TO MADRID- "A"
MADRID TO BARCELONA- "B"
MADRID-CORDOBA, GRANADA, SEVILLE-"C"
THE COSTA DEL SOL- "D"
BILBAO, SAN SABASTIAN, SANTIAGO DE COMPOSTELA- "E" (SDC)
BARCELONA TO PARIS- "F"
MADRID-LISBON- "G"

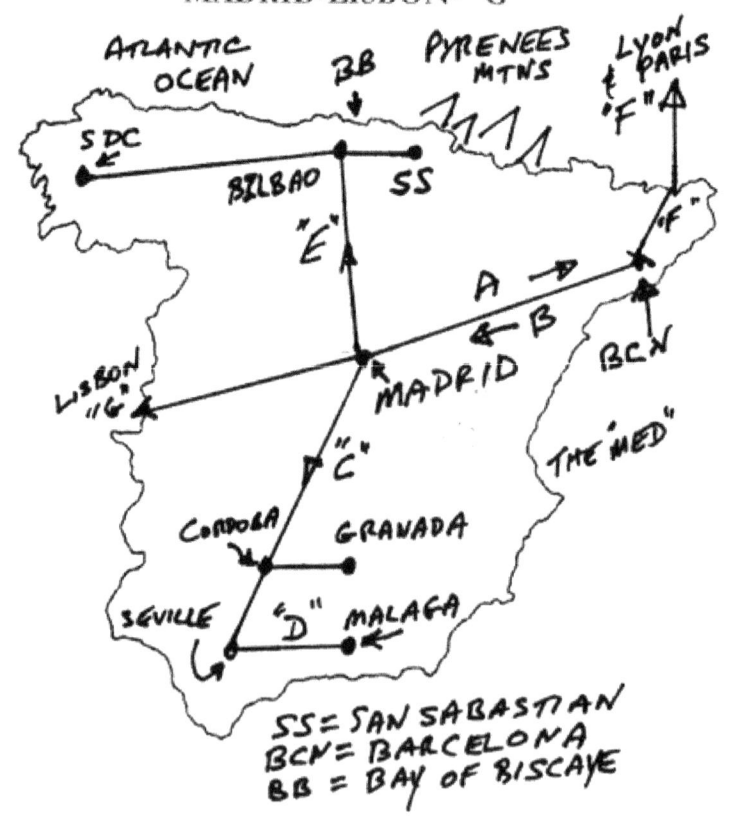

SS= SAN SABASTIAN
BCN= BARCELONA
BB = BAY OF BISCAYE

INTRODUCTION

SPAIN.. THE BEST PLACES TO SEE BY RAIL
AN ALTERNATIVE TO THE ESCORTED TOUR

****STOP*** Before you read this introduction, I would suggest you read the section toward the end of this chapter first, *"HOW TO USE THIS BOOK"*. You will save a lot of time and energy planning your visit to Spain and eliminating all the confusion and stress.

WHAT THIS BOOK IS & WHAT IT IS NOT
This book, like my first book, *"Italy..The Best Places to See by Rail, an Alternative to the Escorted Tour,"* is about seeing Spain using the Spanish high-speed rail system (HSR) instead of taking one of those escorted tours, which are bus tours (we called them coaches and not buses). I was in that "fully escorted tour business" for over 30 years. Fifteen years ago, it was the only way to see Spain, unless you wanted to rent a car and drive all over the country.

At that time, most of Spain had a minimal high-speed rail system. It wasn't until 2008 when Spain initiated high-speed rail service between the two major cities of Madrid and Barcelona. Spain woke up very late in the 20th Century in building a high-speed rail network, which I might note now rivals only China with over 2000 miles of high-speed track.

New rail lines have been built from scratch and new stations to meet the growing tourist demand. So, now given this option, you can see the highlights of Spain by whizzing through the Spanish countryside at speeds of almost 250 miles per hour, which is quite impressive. And to boot, a week or ten days in Spain via rail will cost you about half of what you would expect to pay for one of those escorted "bus" tours.

This book is about just that. How you plan a rail tour and then how you enjoy it. It is not a compilation of rail schedules, costs, etc. You can quickly get that information on the internet. What I have done in this book is provide you with suggested itineraries for one, two, three, or four weeks in Spain. I offer you what a bus tour company would provide you with, except it's by rail, and it's easy. And no, you don't have to lug your bags all over the place!

For each itinerary, I provide you with a day-by-day "what to see and do." Also, I weave into each day's activities, how to get there by train with tips on what time of the day you should depart your base city of

Barcelona, Madrid, Cordoba, etc., and what time you should return to your base city. Let's face it, who wants to waste precious time checking in and out of hotels only to hear, "I'm sorry your room is not ready."

Suppose this is your second or third visit to Spain. In that case, you may want to consider "Itinerary C," which originates in Madrid and goes on to the significant historical cities and sites in "Andalusia," which is south of the Plain of Spain usually referred to as Castile a/k/a "La Mancha" from Don Quixote. The three key cities visited are Granada, Cordoba, and Seville. Unlike Madrid and Barcelona, these cities are what I call "ancient." They are old! Most of them date to the Medieval era of Europe, and even some have their roots in the remnants of the Roman Empire. Most of them are walled cities with castles (called Alcazars), knights in shining armor, and yes, Don Quixote and his trusted squire, Sancho Panza.

Also in Andalusia lies the "Costa Del Sol" (CDS), starting in Malaga to the east and going westward along the Mediterranean toward the major city of Marbella. Miles and miles of high-rise condominiums and resort hotels line the beaches of Torremolinos, Fuengirola, Benalmadena, Mijas, and all those little towns between them. These resort areas are also steeped in history with lots of "see and dos."

The central city and home to the airport that serves the area, Malaga (AGP), is still partially walled. It is home to one of the Picasso museums, which is worth a visit.

About one hour past Marbella going west, you will find the small country of Gibraltar, once a British colony. Yes, that's where the rock is and all those monkeys. This place is definitely worth a day trip. I have devoted a whole section to it and how to get there by bus (coach) in about one hour from the CDS area. There is no direct train service to Gibraltar or the Spanish border city of La Linea de Concepcion.

Did you know you can be in three continents (North America, Europe and Africa) in one week? I have devoted an entire chapter to visiting Tangier, Morocco for a day. You can do this from Seville or cities in the Costa del Sol area. I explain all the ways, time of travel and costs associated with visiting Morocco for the day.

And no trip to the Costa del Sol is complete without a day trip to Ronda, home of the first bullfight and its 300-foot deep gorge. This place is incredible for shopping. It's our favorite place in all of Spain for shopping! Ladies, if you want those knee-high leather boots, this is the place. And, men, if you are looking for shoes and other leather items, yes, this is the place for you! I describe all your options for a day trip to Ronda.

If you have been to Andalusia, Madrid, the Costa del Sol, and Barcelona, you may want to consider a week or ten days in the Basque Country and visit San Sebastian and Bilbao. If you do not know about Bilbao, it is the home of one of the five Guggenheim Museums in the world. It's not the art in the museum, which is the draw for millions of people each year; it is the building itself. Yes, that's right. It is a creation of the 21st Century's most notable architect, Frank Gehry. There is no question here; it is the building itself, which is the most impressive work of art "in" the museum.

On the western side above Portugal lies Santiago de Compostela in the Spanish region known as Galicia. Translated into English, it means the "Burial Ground of St. James." It is one of the leading Catholic shrines, right up there with Lourdes, Fatima, and the others.

And in summary, with the exception of few day trips, all of these places to visit are easily reached by train. Most of them are reached by the new high speed rail network.

WHAT THIS BOOK IS NOT
If you are looking for a detailed book for touring Spain, this is not the book for you. You can find loads and loads of books on Spain on Amazon.com and through popular book sellers worldwide. This book is different. I don't describe all the attractions you can visit in Madrid or the detailed history of Seville. I also do not

provide you with a detailed description of hotels and restaurants in the towns and cities I cover in this book. However, I do include hotels in and around the rail stations, which require only a ten-minute or so walk. Once again, there are plenty of books which do all this. In addition to this book, you will need to purchase one of those "other" books to supplement this book.

Further, don't look to this book as a rail guide to getting anywhere in Spain. It isn't. It won't tell you which train to take to visit your aunt in Zamora. Once again, it's written for the tourist who wants to visit Spain, doesn't want to take a pricey escorted tour, or waste his/her time driving around on those scary high-speed roads. You could also be caught in one of those "alleys" of the medieval cities that you managed to jam your rental car into, and the only exit is to hoist you out.

The itineraries I have constructed in this book are not rigid. What I mean by that is you can easily add one, two, or three days while you are in a major "base" for additional day trips. I provide details on all these day trips in separate chapters.

A WORD ABOUT MY "TIPS"
If you have read my book "*Italy... The Best Places to See by Rail, An Alternative to the Escorted Tour*", you will know about my TIPS comments. For example, assuming you are going from Barcelona to Madrid on

the AVE train (which makes the run in 2.5 hours), you want to take a morning train at about 9 AM. Why? In this way, you can visit the Prado or walk the streets of Old Madrid after you check into your hotel at about 1 PM. Or did you know that the Prado (one of the most famous museums in the world, on par with the Louvre of Paris) is free after 6 PM? If you are traveling from Madrid to Barcelona, you want to take an evening train around 7 PM. In this way it allows you to spend the day in Toledo, Avila or Segovia instead of wasting it on a train. Now, who would have thought about that?

Oh yes, if you want to have dinner in the oldest restaurant in the world... "Casa Botin," you will have to make a reservation at least six weeks in advance. And, do request a table in the "cellar." You can also look at my tips in terms of "insider information." You won't usually find these tips on the internet or any of those travel books you can buy on the shelves of the mega book stores or your favorite book store.

HOW TO USE THIS BOOK
Okay, you bought this book because you didn't want to take one of those pricey escorted tours or drive around in a country where you felt uncomfortable. Most importantly, you knew you wanted to visit Spain but hadn't the foggiest idea on what to see and do. All you knew is perhaps Madrid was the capital and Barcelona was a fun place to visit because you watched the Woody

Allen film "*Vicky Cristina Barcelona*." You probably also knew a little about the historic cities of Seville, Cordoba, and Granada. Great, now we're on the right track (funny) and ready to plan our visit to Spain. That's what this book is all about.

I have always felt that one third of a trip is planning it, one-third is doing it, and the final third is remembering all the things you did, "time and money should make memories." Now comes the fun, the planning.

Take a cursory look at this book. Get one of those travel guides to Spain, figure out how many days you want to visit, and roughly what your budget will be. You will also need a detailed map of Spain. I recommend the Michelin country maps. If you are a AAA or a CAA member, you can obtain maps from them. AAA Plus members usually do not pay for international maps or tour books. Oh yes, you will need a yellow highlighter.

Forgetting the airfare, you can budget for a couple (not per person) $250-300 per day for rail, three-star hotels, and meals. If you are traveling solo, you can figure $200-$250 per day. And yes, if you care to spend more and stay at four and five-star hotels, you can and likewise for staying at hostels.

My suggestion to everyone who is making their first trip to Spain is to visit Madrid and Barcelona. As discussed later in this book, if you anticipate a Mediterranean cruise, I suggest you skip Barcelona and visit Madrid and the south, "Andalusia." That should fill two weeks. So best to just lay out what places you want to see and, just as they say, "connect the dots." My rail itineraries make this so simple.

If you have any comments, corrections, or items that I should include in a subsequent edition, please email me at thegelatopress@gmail.com

THE GEOGRAPHY OF SPAIN

Spain is unique; they placed the capital and the hub of the entire rail system in the country's geographic center. So all trains funnel in and out of Madrid. For example, if you are in Toledo (40 miles southwest of Madrid) and want to go to Malaga (on the Mediterranean), you must go back to Madrid and transfer to a train for Malaga. It is very much like the US airline's hub and spoke system. Well, if you are doing anything of a long-haul nature, you must go back to Madrid. However, only recently has the Spanish government done something about this. They have now added what I call a "Madrid Bypass," so you can go from Barcelona to Seville without going through Madrid. This routing is quite common in Italy, where trains from Naples to Florence can altogether bypass Rome. As tourism grows, watch for more of this.

EUROS, MILES, KILOMETERS AND TIME

All amounts in this book that are expressed as dollars are meant to mean US dollars. I also use Euros very frequently to get you to think in terms of Euros. As of this writing, the bank exchange rate of dollars to Euros is about 1.22. This means that you will need to give up $1.22 to buy one Euro. I explain more conversions in the chapter on money, telephone calls, security, etc.

Similar to money, I use miles and kilometers interchangeably. To get you use to dealing with kilometers, I may express a distance in miles and sometimes in kilometers or sometimes both ways. For example, sometimes, I may express a train ride of about 40 miles. Other times I may express that same 40 miles as 64 kilometers. It's easy to convert back and forth. Just multiply kilometers by .62 to get miles.

In terms of time, most schedules and sometimes admission times use the 24 hours, or sometimes called military time. Using the 24-hour clock or military time eliminates the confusion of AM and PM. So if you see a time of departure of 14:30, that would be 2:30 PM. To convert to PM, subtract 12 from the number stated.

Also, bear in mind that Spain adheres to Daylight Savings Time. However, they do not change times on the exact dates as the USA. Spain changes times the last Sunday in March and the last Sunday in October.

If you are taking the trains, it is best to verify with your hotel concierge the correct time if you are traveling over the last weekends of March or October.

CHANGING TIMES AND TICKETS

Because of COVID, and it's always a good habit, I always verify train times, museum times, etc., in the planning stage of a trip. You don't want to arrive at the Prado museum on a Monday only to find out it's closed.

You should note that when I quote either the price of a rail ticket or an entrance fee to an attraction, it is usually a "ballpark" figure. So you may expect to pay eight Euros for the entrance to The Prado, or it may be ten Euros. I am sure you get the point.

In many cases, when taking taxi rides to the rail stations, I provide a range of prices, with comments like "from the Hotel Puerta de Toledo to Atocha station the taxi fare will be 4-6 Euros". And remember we don't usually tip a taxi driver in Spain, but it's okay to say "keep the change" (I mean the coins, one Euro or less).

Also, plan your "long haul" rail journeys and remember to purchase those tickets as soon as they go online. And, do the same for your attractions i.e., The Alhambra, The Prado, etc.

And finally, before you buy those rail tickets, see my chapter on the Eurail passes. Unlike Italy, there may be more substantial savings with a *Spain* Eurail pass.

A WORD ABOUT RAILEUROPE.COM

In 2020, due to the massive COVID pandemic, the Raileurope.com organization based in Westchester, NY, and a suburb of Chicago shuttered its doors to travelers and travel agents. It existed for over 80 years. Rail Europe was a consortium of European railroads headed by Swiss Rail. Because of the severe and rapid turndown of traveling to Europe, the organization laid off all employees and terminated service to the public in early 2020. However, that said, SNCF, the French Railway operator, stepped in to continue the operation as the new Raileurope (now called Raileurope SAS). Services are mainly online now. However, best you try to book directly via RENFE.com, the dominant Spanish railway company.

Just a note in passing. While I may recommend certain hotels and restaurants, I receive no compensation from them. Nada.... not even a free meal or a one-night stay!

A NOTE ABOUT THE COVID-19 PANDEMIC

Like Italy, Spain has dramatically reduced their intercity train schedules during the pandemic crisis. Where there were once five trains a day from Cordoba to Granada, you will only find three now. As the pandemic dissipates, hopefully, RENFE will add more trains to their inter-city schedules.

From my review, the number of commuter trains, as opposed to AVE intercity trains, has not been reduced significantly. Therefore, your schedule of rail day trips out of Madrid (Cercanias trains) and Barcelona (Rodalies trains) should not be affected.

>>>TIP<<<
AND ONE FINAL TIP ABOUT RAIL SCHEDULES
Yes, they do tend to change, but rarely. It is best to check with your hotel concierge at least a day or two before your next rail journey if the schedule has changed. He will look it up in a minute on the Renfe schedule. The worst thing is to arrive at the station and find that your inter-city AVE train at 9 AM has been canceled, and all you see on the station is the words "SEE AGENT." Gee, if I had known that sooner, I would have re-booked on the earlier train at 7 AM.
>>>>><<<<<

A WORD ABOUT CHICAGO MANUAL OF STYLE
The poet "E.E. Cummings", did not believe in the Chicago Manual. Neither do I. You will find many violations, which allows me to make this book more user-friendly. For example, instead of writing, "The AVE train takes two hours and thirty minutes to cover the distance from Barcelona to Madrid," I say, "it's about a 2.5 hour run from Barcelona to Madrid."

CHAPTER 1

SPAIN, SPAIN, SPAIN
IT'S A "SLEEPER"

INTRODUCTION

Second, only to Italy, this is my favorite country in Western Europe. As a frequent traveler to both countries, I love them both! Like Italy, Spain is steeped in history. The people, like the Italians, are warm. In my opinion, the cuisine is second only to Italy. If you like what Italy has to offer you will love Spain. I don't know what it is, but Spain does not get the "play" Italy does. Everyone wants to go to Italy, but few jump to spend a few weeks in Spain.

I'm a little partial anyway to Spain. My great ancestors on my father's side came from Spain. My dad always said the family probably came from Toledo, but it could have been anywhere in Spain. Perhaps it was Cordoba, Girona, Seville, or somewhere else. Nobody knows. Now a short history of Spain. You should consult those big fat and heavy tour books for more details.

They called it Iberia before there were countries. Iberia was all the land south of the Pyrenees' Mountains on that massive peninsula south of France. You should not confuse this with the "Kingdom of Iberia," which is sometimes referred to as Eastern Iberia, which dates to about 500BC and is located over 4000 miles away next to Armenia and present-day Iran. This Eastern Iberia Kingdom was part of the Persian empire. The land 4000 miles away from present-day Spain is not the Iberia we know of today.

It is believed the earliest inhabitants of the Iberian Peninsula date to about 600BC. The Greeks, the Romans, Moors, Arabs, and several dozen civilizations made their mark on this diverse land. I won't bore you with any more history since you will need about a year to read all the details of Iberia. And yes, the airline of Spain is known as Iberian Airlines.

About the year 1000AD, countries began to form on the Iberian Peninsula. Today we know it as Spain and Portugal. There are two other countries which exist on the peninsula. Andorra, one of the smallest countries in the world, dates to about the same time frame as the founding of Spain. It's only about 200 square miles and is high up in the Pyrenees between Spain and France. The other is Gibraltar, which has been part of the British Commonwealth of Nations since 1730.

When one thinks of Spain, what comes to your mind? Don Quixote or is it the "The rain in Spain stays mainly in the plain" from *My Fair Lady*? Perhaps it's Seville, or is it that in Barcelona, they speak Catalan and the rest of Spain speaks Spanish? Maybe it's that Paella dinner followed by the Flamenco show in Seville that piques your interest.

Oh, I forgot to mention the area to the Northeast corner of Spain known as the Basque Country (up against France and the Atlantic) where they speak "Basque." Basque is a jabberwocky type of language. In other words, you don't pronounce it like an English or Latin word. For example, the words "pleased to meet you" are "Pozten naiz zu ezagutzeaz" . That being said, you will want to visit Bilbao, the home of the Guggenheim Museum of Europe. Forget about the museum itself; it's the building that makes this a world-famous site to visit. And yes, it's all reachable by train.

It seems high-speed auto ways and trains in Spain have always lagged behind other countries in Western Europe. I remembered my first trip to Spain in 1972. It took me a whole day to drive from Madrid to Malaga (on the Costa del Sol) on a dusty two-lane highway. It took another 15 years to develop the "A" type road system, similar to our Eisenhower interstate highway system in the United States.

Before, the high speed (TGV type bullet trains) arrived on the scene, Spanish trains were slooooo (sic), rickety rackety, and dusty. They were still using steam locomotives until 1975. It wasn't until the mid '80's that the government of Spain decided to do what the other countries of Europe had done already, build a high-speed rail (HSR) network connecting the major cities and the historical sites, e.g., Cordoba, Toledo, etc.

They took their time and slowly expanded the system. It was not until 2004 that the high-speed AVE (Alta Velocity Espana) trains started running between Barcelona and Madrid.

Spain now has the second-largest rail network only next to China. There are over 2000 miles of high-speed lines. The fastest trains travel at about 200 miles per hour.

While the Government of Spain owns the rail network (Adif), most trains, especially the high-speed ones, AVE, AVANT, and ALVIA, are operated by Renfe, also known as Renfe Operadora. In May of 2021, a compcting operator from France, SNCF (the originator of the TGV bullet train between Paris and Lyon), will also offer high-speed rail service between Madrid and Barcelona and other points in Spain.

The company, a subsidiary of SNCF, will be known as OUIGO and will start service in the Spring of 2021. It is rumored that the cost of the high-speed AVE type trains will be about half that of Renfe. They will only offer tourist class seating with vending machines instead of a club or café car.

Renfe, now in conjunction with the French rail operator SNCF offers high-speed rail service to Paris, Lyon, and Perpignan. More of this is explained in the chapter "The French Connection."

Other operators offer local service or regional service within Spain. I will inform you of these when discussing the suggested itineraries. In the same way, I did in my book *"ITALY... The Best Places to See by Rail an alternative to the escorted tour"*, also available at Amazon, Barnes & Noble, and other booksellers in the US, Canada, and the United Kingdom.

What I like best about Spain is that a one, two, or three-week visit will allow you to take in medieval cities, modern museums and finish it off with a week on one of the beaches of the Costa del Sol. I don't know of any other country in Western Europe which can offer you this "diversity."

No question, Italy gets the play. But few people know about Spain. Ask anyone if you know about the Coliseum in Rome or the canals of Venice. They will all say yes and have pictures in their mind. Ask them about any of the sites in Spain, and they haven't the foggiest clue. They won't know where the Mezquita is and, let alone, won't even know what it is. Likewise, for the Alhambra (not the Ala-hambra) and what it is. Mention the Guggenheim, and most people will say, "I visited it several years ago in New York." However, I would say most of them are clueless about what's in Spain and where it's located.

Furthermore, very few people know about Spain's cuisine, or should I say the regional cuisines of Spain. Most people will tell you, "I love Paella and Sangria." Okay, that's fine, but have you tried the roast dishes of Madrid and the Basque country. Have you tried Tapas? I can tell you it's better than Chinese Dim Sum. Nothing beats a day of sightseeing, dropping into your local café or bar about 5 PM, enjoying a glass of wine and a selection of Tapas, then getting back to your hotel for a nap and shower before dinner at eight.

The best thing I like about dinner is that you get to enjoy all those regional specialties when you travel from region to region (via the train, of course). While I love pasta in Italy, I want a roast one night in Madrid and a seafood dish on the coast the next day in Seville. Nothing beats an appetizer of cold tomato soup (Gazpacho Andaluz) in Cordoba after a hot day of trekking around the Old City.

Oh, did I tell you about those scrumptious Spanish breakfasts? They're not the typical deluxe continental breakfast you enjoy in Italy, France, or Greece. First, Spaniards love their Jambon (ham), and it's cured several ways. So do expect a selection, and yes, the cheeses. Their rolls, artisan breads and pastries are excellent, many with custards in them. And let's not forget those great olives. One of my favorites every morning is the Tortilla de Patatas. It's a large potato and egg omelet. It's not the tortilla you know from Mexico. It's completely different. Did I mention those churros you dip in hot chocolate, which has the consistency of chocolate pudding, or great pastries?

And what I like most about a rail tour, you are never rushed! If you want to make that 11 AM train to Toledo and enjoy your breakfast, you can. No rushing to get on the bus at 8 AM when it rolls to Toledo, with a group of 50 other travelers. The day becomes less stressful and more leisurely. And, don't forget more time to shop! And best of all it will cost you a lot less than one of those fully escorted and highly regimented tours.

In this book, I explain how to visit the different regions of the country. Starting in Barcelona or Madrid, then moving on to Andalusia (Cordoba, Granada, and Seville) and, if you have a few more weeks, a visit to the Costa del Sol area. If you want to travel to Northern Spain, you can visit Bilbao, home of the Guggenheim

Museum, San Sabastian and Santiago d Compostela, all by train while you take in the views of the countryside from the plains to the mountains to the oceans. Spain's got it all!

Read on and get ready to plan for a visit to Spain!

CHAPTER 2

FOUR WAYS TO VISIT SPAIN

INTRODUCTION

There are four ways to visit Spain: 1) The escorted tour; 2) the FIT or commonly known as Foreign Independent Travel; 3) a private car with a driver, and; 4) a rail tour. It breaks down to the time you have available and the adventure pleasure, i.e., enjoyment you wish to have. Couple this with how much money you want to spend, and you will have the perfect Spanish holiday vacation, as they say. Forget about an inland waterways tour of Spain as a first-time trip. There are none. Don't consider a Mediterranean cruise to see Spain. You usually will only see Barcelona. Spain's rich history and beauty are found in its "ancient" (medieval period) inland cities like Toledo, Seville, Segovia, Avila, Cordoba, and Granada. I consider Madrid and Barcelona, along with Bilbao and the other cities, relatively "modern." Yes, they do have their old sections like Valencia, but they lack that medieval way and those small cobblestone streets, or should I say alleys, which will take you back sometimes almost 1000 or more years.

The first way to see Spain as you would Italy, and what I believe to be the easiest, i.e., with no hassles, is the escorted tour. I recommend this type of tour if you are not going to do it FIT (Foreign Independent Travel) or a rail tour, which this book is all about. However, you will see below that the rail tour offers you more in terms of flexibility and leisure in addition to dramatic savings over an escorted "bus" tour. Let's look at the pros and cons of an escorted tour.

ESCORTED TOURS

Many years ago, Greyhound Bus lines had the slogan "relax and leave the driving to us." This saying is so true with escorted tours. They usually include all hotels and breakfasts for each day on tour in addition to the services of a state-certified tour guide. Many times they also include what they call porterage. So all you need to do is go to your room, and your bags are usually delivered within an hour. Waiting for your luggage gives you some time to take a snooze or a power nap or perhaps have a drink at the lobby bar.

One additional benefit of an escorted tour is that many operators provide transfers that allow you to reach your first hotel on tour without a $200 taxi ride! There is usually a "meet and greet" person at the airport after you clear customs and immigration, holding a sign with your name. They arrange for your transport with your bags to your hotel—no need to lug them.

Once the tour starts, you will be using Spanish coaches (we don't call them buses). They all have toilets (for emergency use) on board. However, there are rest stops on the major roads with plenty of clean facilities, snack bars, and souvenirs every few miles. Most coaches stop every hour or two for a break. Smoking is not allowed on touring coaches. Unlike the United States, Spain is certainly geared up for tourism.

Since I owned and operated a fully escorted tour company for almost thirty years, I can tell you that they are highly regimented. We always had a saying with my group tour company National Travel Vacations: "What are 6, 7, and 8?" No, it wasn't a question from the CBS TV show "Jeopardy"! It means 6 AM, wake-up call, 7 AM breakfast, and 8 AM the coach departs. The entire day is touring on an exact itinerary (knowing hour by hour where you would be) with lots of historical narration. Stops are made for lunch and snacks (sometimes included). Since it's Spain, we check into our hotel and then go to dinner at about 8 PM. It is a rigorous and tiring long day, but you do see a lot.

Depending on the tour schedule that day (we call it the "timing"), there is some free time i.e., shopping in Toledo for some Damascene earrings or a small pillbox or whatever. However, if you want another hour or two to buy some stocking stuffers for Christmas, forget it! You have got to be back on that coach else, take a taxi back to Madrid. Sometimes there is even a free whole day on your own. Gee, what would I do?

Also, tour operators obtain group tickets for museums, and other attractions, thus eliminating the need for a group to stand in line, perhaps at the Royal Palace in Madrid or the General Life in Granada.

In summary, the tour is highly regimented. However, on the plus side, you have to do absolutely nothing except enjoy yourself. These tours are best enjoyed by seniors who don't want any hassle or anything strenuous, either mentally or physically. Just no stress.

UPSELLING THE TOUR
So you paid $899 for that Madrid-Barcelona nine-day tour which also, I might note, contained two free days. On arrival at the hotel on the "gathering day," you probably will have a wine and cheese reception or a meet and greet with the other members of your group. You will also meet your tour director for the week. After you are into your second glass of Sangria, you will hear about those two extra day trips… wowy, wowy. Yes, if you want to go to Segovia and Avila for the day, including lunch, it will cost you another $150, the same for a day trip to Toledo. Now, what are you doing for dinner each night? That will be another $200 for the seven-night dinner plan. And yes, they will throw in a one-hour Flamenco show after dinner, including one

free drink. So be prepared to take out your credit card and charge another $500 per person for those extra's. It's just like the shore excursions on a cruise. There is nothing wrong with this. However, many guests on tour had no idea they were not going to Toledo, Avila, or Segovia, all less than one hour from Madrid. The same goes for Montserrat and Girona in the Barcelona area. These "baseline" tours are really "glorified" city tours unless you opt for those extras.

FOREIGN INDEPENDENT TRAVEL
The second way of seeing Spain is known as Foreign Independent Travel or FIT. FIT is where you book your hotels, rent a car, and do all those other good things i.e., get your General Life (Alhambra-Granada) tickets online, etc. However, renting a car and driving in Spain is very much like Italy. It creates high levels of stress and may even cause a divorce (just kidding). Forget driving in places like Toledo or Avila with those tiny (narrow) cobblestone streets. I almost got stuck physically in an alley in Toledo with my rental car, no kidding. I had to slide out of the alley with about a quarter of an inch on each side of my rental.

On a positive note, the highway system in Spain is up to par with Italy. However, with the exception of a few toll areas (known as "AP" roads), most of the inter-city roads are toll-free. There are exceptions like the Madrid-Barcelona toll road. However, the drivers, very much like Italy, are very aggressive and border on "crazy." The Spaniards like to drive fast. So if you drive in that fast lane, be prepared to have someone on your tail (wearing sunglasses, of course) in a few seconds trying to get you out of the left high-speed lane so he can move on with his business. It's quite intimidating, to say the least. As in Italy, this type of aggressive driving on intercity roads is also the norm in Spain.

FIT eliminates the regimentation of an escorted tour; however, you still have to do all the driving around the country, assuming you can rent a car. Also, you will have to figure how to park in many cities and at attractions. Parking is usually non-existent in many medieval towns. You usually will have to park in parking lots or garages several blocks from your in-city hotel. You should also be aware that many rental companies will not rent to visitors below 25 or above 80. Oh, I forgot to tell you about the gas issue. Gas (Petro, fuel, diesel) costs about $7 per gallon. A fill-up for a small car will usually cost about $70. As of this writing, the average is about 1.40 Euro per liter. With four liters to the gallon approximately and given the exchange rate of $1.25 figure yes… the $7 per gallon. The gas from Madrid to Barcelona will cost you about $150 and let's not forget the $45 for the tolls.

In summary, you can attempt to drive, but be aware that you need to get a prescription for Valium. You will need to take two each day, one at breakfast and one before you retire for the evening.

Oh, I did forget to mention the most important item. The trains traverse the distance you would have driven in a rental car in one-third the time. In the Madrid-Barcelona corridor, what would take a car eight hours (with stops, of course) takes the high-speed AVE train only two hours and thirty minutes. Saving time using the high-speed trains alone will save you an entire day and allow this day for sightseeing instead of "white knuckle driving."

It's a lot of work but can be a lot of fun as you plan the entire itinerary. The internet has made this fun and straightforward. You plan the day-to-day places you want to be and the sights you want to visit. You then decide on the hotels. However, you will need time to get lost in each city and find your way to your hotel, even with a good GPS unit. You will waste time checking in and checking out. And, finally, there is a lot of stress; not to mention stashing your chariot for the night somewhere. As another alternative, you can hire a driver and a private car for your entire visit. And, yes, you need to reserve a room for your driver each night. So read on.

PRIVATE CAR WITH DRIVER

If you have the financial means to do it, the third alternative is the private car with a driver. You can scour the internet for these services and work directly with either the car agency in Spain or a travel agent in the USA or Canada who will take care of everything. You can figure about $1000- $1500 per day per person for five-star hotels, driver, car, meals, gratuities, and incidentals. The cost also includes the room and meals for your driver. This option is usually for those "A list" people or seniors who wish to spend their kid's inheritance now instead of when they pass on.

Here we are with the fourth alternative, which many people do not know about in the USA and Canada who are used to taking those "escorted tours." So here we go with the rail tour.

A RAIL TOUR THROUGH SPAIN

The fourth alternative and the subject of this book are the benefits and enjoyment of a rail tour through Spain. This book explains how to plan your Spain rail vacation with ease. But first, lct's look at the Spanish rail system compared to the rail system in the USA.

When I chat with people on this subject, they say, "you mean I am going to take the train around Spain?" You have to be kidding! They usually make a quick comparison with our Amtrak (USA) system or the Canadian system known as "Via Rail".

Unlike the American rail system, the Spanish railway infrastructure was built and is owned by the federal government. Ownership of the rail system (not the trains) gives the Spanish government complete control over the operation of their trains and the new competitive train company from France known as "Ouigo." There is quite a difference between the USA, where, with the Northeast Corridor (NEC) exception, Amtrak uses private railroad tracks owned by the large freight railroads and not the government, i.e., CSX, Union Pacific, etc., to operate their trains.

Even though Amtrak trains are given priority over freight trains, they usually, except for the NEC, run several hours dramatically late. Delays of several hours to a full day late are rampant. On the other hand, Spanish passenger trains run right on the clock. If you are running late for a train and arrive about one minute after the published departure time, you will find the train has departed. It is rare that trains ever run more than five minutes behind schedule. Don't compare taking a slow and delayed Amtrak train across America with taking a rail trip through Spain. They are different.

Look at the cover of this book. That sleek *AVE* train will make the run from Madrid to Barcelona in two hours 30 minutes. That's the distance between Boston and Washington. Even Amtrak's "high-speed" Acela will take almost four times longer.

If you don't believe it, here is a quick summary-
Google Maps:
AMTRAK BOS-WASHINGTON   439 MILES 9.5HRS
RENFE MADRID-BARCELONA 437 MILES 2.5 HRS

In summary, there is absolutely no comparison between Amtrak and the AVE type trains of Spain. They are a world apart.

There is another benefit of having the federal government (ADIF in Spain) own the tracks. It means you will now choose which railway company to travel between several of the major cities. This choice is now available in Italy and will be available shortly in Spain. The competition gives the consumer a lower price for the service and more frequent schedules, if you just want to get from point A to point B without any amenities, this is the way to go for the tourist. This service will be very similar to Easy Jet and Ryan Air, the economy (discount) air carriers in Europe.

Taking what I call a rail tour is simple, easy, enjoyable, relaxing, and a lot of fun. However, many people don't know it exists or even know how to use it. If they are interested in seeing Spain, the first thing that comes to mind is an escorted tour. However, unlike the other ways described above, a rail tour offers the benefits of no regimentation coupled with a dramatically lower cost for the vacation and little or no stress. It certainly is a cost-effective alternative to the escorted tour, with many additional benefits. And no, you don't have to lug your bags. When the taxi driver comes to your hotel, he will put those bags in the taxi. You need not even offer to help. Once you get to the rail station, there are porters there who will lug your bags to the train platform. It is easy. All you need to do is have a few Euros in your pocket for those tips.

Here is a quick summary of the four types of vacations by regimentation, cost and stress level:

VACATION	REGI	COST/DAY	STRESS
Escorted Bus Tour (1)	High	$300-500	None
FIT w/Rental Car (2)	None	$200	High
Private Car w/driver (3)	None	$1000-1500 (4)	None
Rail Tour	None	$150	Little

Notes:
Airfare is excluded, REGI means regimentation
Cost/Day is per person (double occupancy).

(1) Includes 4-star hotels with breakfast, lunch and some dinners, extra tours, tips, etc. Costs can be much higher with top-of-the-line tour operators who may include all meals, tips, etc.
(2) Includes rental car, insurance, gas, tolls, parking.
(3) Includes cost also of a single room and driver meals.
(4) This is for a couple, not per person.
All four options include admissions to museums and other places of interest.

While we are at it, I will describe the benefits of train travel on a Renfe AVE class train. Note, many of the older AVE trains may lack some of the amenities listed:

AVE (Preferente Class) First class ultra-clean toilets just like the airlines;
    Power receptacles for charging phones;
    Video Monitors and background music;
    Luggage racks;
    Wi-Fi;
    A meal and beverage;
    Use of the first class lounge before departure

AVE Tourista Plus
    Many of the above features, except no meals.
On all other trains which are not AVE *Class*, restrooms are usually included in mid-train.

QUICK REVIEW

High-speed rail travel (almost 200MPH) allows fast transit with little or no stress between major points in Spain. Fast transit will enable you to take a morning train and enjoy the balance of the day instead of driving a rental car or sitting in a bus. You can also take what I call a sunset train, thus allowing you to enjoy the day and then relax en route to your next destination. The Spanish high-speed rail system will enable you to do all this in comfort. I explain all this in detail: trains to take, what to see and do and even hotels near the rail stations, so you don't have to take taxis all over town.

So, let's read on.

To avoid costly airline, change fees, remember to read this book first, cover to cover. Before getting those airline tickets, do your detailed planning by connecting those dots on the maps and figuring how many days you will need in each locale. You may want to add a "buffer" of 2-3 extra days just if you need it. So if you layout your 12-day trip, add those two additional days. I don't know how many people I have met that always say "I needed two more days, guess I will do it on the next trip to Spain."

CHAPTER 3

CRITICAL THINGS TO DO BEFORE WE GO

PASSPORTS

You will definitely need a passport, but no visa is required if you are staying less than 90 days. And yes, you do not need any shots from your doctor. Best to make a few copies of your passport and put them in your bags should they go astray. You can also take a picture of it and stash it in your smart-phone. It is suggested that you have at least six months validity before your passport expires, otherwise most countries will not let you enter. So if your passport expires, May 1, 2022, you cannot travel to Spain (and other countries) in April, 2022. You must get it renewed.

COVID NOTICE

The rules for travel under the COVID pandemic keep on changing. You should contact the Spanish travel office at travelsafe.spain.info/en/ or travelsafe-abroad.com/spain/ and of course the US State Department at travel.state.gov/content/travel.html.

INTERCITY RAIL TICKETS

It's best to purchase your intercity rail tickets on Renfe.com. or Ouigo.com. If you want, consider taking the hassle out of the booking by calling the new *Raileurope.com* in the USA. They provide excellent advice and will book your reservations and provide your tickets for you. However, bear in mind that their prices and schedules sometimes do not include all the intercity trains and rail companies and, secondly most of the time they do add a small booking fee in addition to other fees i.e. express delivery of your tickets, etc. However, their effort is certainly worth the booking fee, and it is one less thing you have to worry about. Also, most tickets for the long-hauls i.e. Madrid to Cordoba, etc. go on sale about 60 days before. In the busy Madrid-Barcelona corridor the tickets go on sale usually 120 days prior. Because of the start up from Ouigo, you may expect this to be increased to 150 days.

Before I call *Raileurope*, I check on-line with Renfe.com to see what their prices are. Consider also using a knowledgeable travel agent that as an agent for the railroads can provide you with information and tickets. Most of them are well versed in intercity travel in Spain, however, they may not know too much about how you get from Antequera to Zamora, let alone where these places are. Also remember that when looking for tickets you must use the Spanish city name i.e. Sevilla.

Using the improper name will return you an error statement— "no such station".

You will not have to purchase rail tickets prior to leaving the USA or Canada for many of the day trips because they are Cercanias (commuter) trains (read the chapters) and not "long-hauls."

FIXED ITINERARY

After you get your outbound and return air tickets, you need to purchase your intercity rail tickets and seat reservations. It will be extremely difficult to cancel or change a rail reservation, unless you purchase a "flex" fare and pay a little extra. Even with a "flex" you may lose a few dollars.

HOTEL RESERVATIONS

When in doubt I always allow for a buffer day here and there. If I can't get that morning train to Cordoba, I can always go the next day. It is far easier to adjust a hotel reservation than a rail reservation. Also, you must always deal directly with the hotel as using an online travel agent (OTA) i.e. Booking.com may not let you change or cancel the reservation if you have chosen one of those "Non-Refundable" rates, because you wanted to save $20. Most hotels will usually allow you to cancel and receive a full refund with a minimum of 7-14 days notice of your anticipated arrival date. Always book directly by obtaining the hotel's official website. Many times OTA's will use devious means to think you are dealing with the hotel directly. For example, do book with santshotel.com (official website) and avoid booking engines (OTA's) which may offer you something in disguise i.e., reservations.sants.com. You may think you are making a booking with the hotel but you are not. You can certainly ask is this the official website of the Sants Hotel in Barcelona? Also, you can ask for a better rate if possible i.e. a senior rate or if taking two or more rooms for a discount. And how about a quiet room or an early arrival?

CRITICAL ADMISSIONS/RESERVATIONS
The Royal Palace (Madrid)
    www.entradas.patrimonionacional.es
Dinner at the Casa Botin- 6-8 weeks prior
The Alhambra (Generalife of Granada) 8-12 weeks prior
Flamenco show in Seville 6 weeks prior
All others you should be able to purchase on the spot
    or on arrival into that city.

Take care of any private car arrangements, airport pickup, car from Seville to Costa del Sol, etc.

NOW THE FINAL POINT
You need to read this entire book and then comeback to this chapter and read it again. Then take care of those critical things.

CHAPTER 4

FIRST LET'S GET TO SPAIN

WHEN TO GO AND FARES

First, consider the seasons. Traveling by train does create another burden in the summer. While you may elect to use porters to carry your bags (not a lot of money), bear in mind that most rail stations and terminals are outdoors and are not air-conditioned. Plan your trip for the summer, and you will have to deal with the scorching heat of Spain, especially Andalusia (Cordoba, Granada, Seville, and the Costa del Sol), where daytime temperatures for July and August will be 110-120 degrees Fahrenheit. I don't want to make lite of this. Spain does have the most extreme summer heat of all the countries in Western Europe. Compare this with London, whose daytime temperatures are about 72 degrees Fahrenheit. Even though all the trains are air-conditioned, the extreme daytime temperature will take a lot out of you, especially if you are a senior.

I would define Spain as beastly hot in the summer, and I mean beastly hot! You should consider the summer as May 15th to October 15th. If you can avoid this time frame, do so. In addition to the hot temperatures, attractions are filled with students and teachers who can usually only take their two-week vacations in the summer months. Attractions, restaurants, and trains also get filled up very early since travelers don't want to be shut out of a morning train from Madrid to Cordoba.

If you are a senior, you may have to stand in line at other attractions and walk a mile or two in the hot sun, especially at the Alhambra in Granada. Trust me. It is very uncomfortable, to say the least. If you are a senior, definitely consider visiting Spain by rail in the cool spring or fall months.

Not only is the heat high, so are the airline tickets. the peak summer months (high season), June through September, fares inbound to Madrid and out of, say, Seville or Malaga are at their highest. In high season, expect to pay up to $1000 for an economy round trip ticket. That same ticket would cost you $400-$700 in the off-season or even less in the late fall and winter.

Also, remember it is also vacation time for the Spaniards. Many will take off for the cooler mountains in the north for a weeks' vacation. So expect some places to be closed, especially restaurants.

Wintertime from November through March is considered the low season. Airfares are at their lowest, and hotels are a bargain.

Wintertime is also excellent if you want to include the Costa del Sol area of Spain. However, remember that you do not want to travel between December 15th and January 10th when the airlines hike the fares up during the holiday season, selling tickets for those wishing to visit friends and family (VFR).

If you are not traveling in the summer months, you will need to take "peel off clothing." It's very much like packing for a trip to San Francisco, where it can be cool during the evening and hot during the day. So if you are visiting Madrid in the winter, expect a minimum of ten degrees warmer in the Costa del Sol area on the Mediterranean. Daily, temperatures in Madrid tend to be about 50 degrees, while Seville may reach nearly 65. So leave that heavy ski parker home and take a fall jack and a sweater or two.

In summary, best to travel during the cool shoulder season or the winter months. You will find tickets for as low as $400 round-trip.

If you are using frequent flyer miles, you will find that many airlines offer what is known as "reduced mileage awards" for flying those winter months. In summary, avoid travel if at all possible during the summer.

BOOKING DIRECT AND PORTALS (OTA)

It is best to book directly with the carrier. You will have more "rights." My suggestion is always to find the flights you want with Momondo, Orbitz, or any portal or OTA (short for Online Travel Agent) where you are comfortable. For Spain, you should be advised that some carriers may not list all their flights within Spain, and further, they may not show up on the "portals." These airlines are Iberia, Vueling, and Air Europa. With respect to "rights," if you are "bumped" on a flight from Madrid to Bilbao on Iberia, and you booked the flight using a portal, you may not be placed on the next flight bound for Bilbao. If you booked directly with Iberia, they would make every attempt to get you to Bilbao even if they have to put you on Air Europa or a Vueling flight. The same is true for seat assignments, lost bags, and special requests, i.e., accommodating persons with physical challenges, etc.

Before purchasing your tickets, do check out and compare the OTA site with the airline's website. Also, consider if you can get your seats on the OTA. Tickets bought on the OTA may not allow seat assignment until you arrive at the gate. Also, if the price drops and you are dealing with the airline directly, they will usually credit back any price difference. Also, remember that some OTAs will not pass along a frequent flyer number. This is another reason for booking directly. So do the research first.

THE MAJOR AMERICAN AIRLINES

Most major American airlines fly from their hubs (New York, Chicago, Atlanta, Philadelphia, Washington DC, etc.) to Madrid, and Barcelona. Because of the COVID-19 pandemic, many airlines have discontinued flying nonstop to both of these cities. Many of the US airlines are flying only nonstop to Madrid. The plane then flies to Barcelona an hour or two later. In the days prior to the pandemic, these US airlines flew nonstops from their US hubs directly to both of these cities. Hopefully, after the pandemic is over, they will re-establish their nonstops to both cities.

All flights to Spain are overnight flights. They depart anywhere from 3 PM for west coast cities to 11 PM for east coast cities and arrive in either Madrid or Barcelona in the early morning. American Airlines (AA) and British Airways (BA) usually offer day flights to London, which allow you to connect with another flight to points in Spain. The only problem is that these flights get into London about 9 PM, and you will usually find that your flight to Seville or Madrid won't take off till 11 AM the following day. An arrival late into one of the London airports will force you to overnight at a hotel until the next day. The nice thing about the day flights offered by these two airlines will usually reduce the jet lag effect on your body. Also, you may not be able to check your bags to your final destination. Best to check with the airline.

FREQUENT FLYER POINTS & 330 DAY RULE

The old saying "the early bird gets the worm." How true this is when trying to use your frequent flyer points. The 330-day rule governs when you can make an airline reservation. What this means is that airlines only allow you to book within 330 days of the departure day. So, you can't book a year out. Bear in mind that you really can't make the booking until your return date is within the 330-day time frame. You can contact the airline and see if they can book the outbound segment. But, you will have to wait a few weeks to book your return.

However, the best is to book as soon as you can and block out your departure date, city, and return. Most rail itineraries discussed favor a fly-in to one city and a fly-out from your final point. So there is no need to go back to Madrid or Barcelona. The concept of flying into one city and out of another is known as an open-jaw itinerary. You may also see it stated as "Multi-City." when you make your booking or use that OTA.

If you are using frequent flyer points, you need to book the outbound and return flights immediately to avoid what I call a "complex routing," which only works to the advantage of the airline. For example, you want to fly JFK to Madrid on American. No problem. However, the JFK flight on that day is booked. Instead, you have to fly from JFK to Charlotte then connect to another flight to Chicago, where you will get your overnight flight to Madrid. Are they kidding? The problem exists because the number of frequent flyer seats on each flight is fixed. Once these are gone, the airline will try to see if they can offer you an alternate routing where frequent flyer seats are available. Yes, if you wanted to pay cash instead of using your frequent flyer points, you could fly JFK to Madrid nonstop. I don't know how many times I had to fly into New York's LaGuardia Airport from Boston and take a taxi for $35 down to JFK because there were no frequent flyer seats available on the 1 PM flight from Boston to JFK.

Here are the suggested inbound/outbound cities:

MADRID-BARCELONA
For first-timers visiting Spain from the USA or Canada, my recommendation is to take the Two Capitals Tour…Barcelona and Madrid, my A/B itinerary. On a tight schedule, you will need 7-10 days to do this. However, if you take your time and add a few days for rest, more shopping, and extra sightseeing, you should figure a full two weeks, including fly days.

Suppose you are going to follow this rail tour; you need to fly into Barcelona and out of Madrid. You can certainly reverse it. However, please take a look at my discussion on Barcelona. In summary, if you have on your bucket list a Mediterranean cruise which will usually originate, terminate or make a stop in Barcelona, skip Barcelona, and fly into Madrid.

>>>TIP<<<
Here is an ultra-critical tip. Please read this book in its entirety first, before you make any airline reservations, where you cannot make any changes or be penalized. Then figure out how much time you have. If this is your first time in Spain, consider one long week. This will allow you to visit Madrid and Barcelona. Again, see my note about taking a cruise out of Barcelona before you consider visiting Barcelona. If you have two "relaxed" weeks, consider the extension to Andalusia, i.e., Cordoba, Granada, and Seville, either from Madrid or Barcelona. If you have another week, enjoy the beaches of Costa del Sol. And, if you have never been to the Basque Country and the Guggenheim, finish your trip in Bilbao or make it your first stop in Spain.
>>>>><<<<<

>>>TIP<<<
Avoid connecting with a flight in London. If you are using frequent flyer miles, the taxes you will pay are "out-of-sight." If you fly nonstop to Madrid, the taxes on a frequent flyer award will be about $85. If you go through London, they will be $450. Yikes! Before booking those "free" tickets, check what the taxes will be. They probably will pay for your hotels in Spain for

the week plus a few dinners. Remember, the flight is free, but you still have to pay those taxes.
>>>>><<<<<

Here are the airlines which fly from the USA to Madrid and Barcelona (before COVID-19 caused curtailments) nonstop. Other airlines use "code shares" in that a KLM flight might be a Delta flight. Check the originating flight time and see any notes on this codeshare. Ticket prices may vary. The others not mentioned fly to Madrid and Barcelona, etc., via their hub cities. Here are the ones who fly nonstop from the USA: American, Iberia, Delta, United, and Air Europa.

Note, to return from Seville or Malaga, in the Costa del Sol, you will have to take one of these airlines and connect in their European hub, or better purchase a one-way ticket back to Madrid or Barcelona or "rail" back via my itineraries. You should note that most Spanish cities have several flights a day operated by Iberia, Air Europa, and Vueling to their hubs in Madrid or Barcelona. For example, Air Europa flies Madrid-Bilbao. You may find limited flights by the other European operators. Vueling and Air Europa, which are based in Spain, are the second and third largest air carriers in the country.

You will find that if you have to return to Madrid or Barcelona for your flight back to North America, your one-way fare will be about $100 and will only take one hour. However, best not to try to connect for your flight back to the USA on the same day. I recommend you fly back to Madrid or Barcelona the night before your flight back to North America. There are numerous hotels around Madrid Airport as well as Barcelona which offer a courtesy shuttle to and from the airport. I recommend the Ibis Hotel in the village of Barajas (it's also the name of the MAD airport). I have stayed there at least six times, and it is ideal. There are numerous restaurants within walking distance of the hotel. An optional breakfast is offered and a free courtesy shuttle.

FLY OUT OF SEVILLE

If you plan on going on to Cordoba, Granada, and terminating your trip in Seville, you can usually fly out of Seville to major hubs in Europe. Therefore, you may want to fly into Madrid or Barcelona and out of Seville. Once again, this is called an "Open Jaw."

FLY OUT OF MALAGA

Malaga (AGP) is the capital of the Costa Del Sol region, also in Andalusia. If you are extending your Spain visit for a week's vacation in many of the Spanish beach resorts, consider flying out of Malaga. It is easily reached by rail from mostly all of the beach communities with the C1 Cercanias line. I describe this C1 line in my chapter on the Costa del Sol.

FLYING OUT OF BILBAO

If you are terminating your stay in Spain in the Basque Country, you should consider flying out of Bilbao (BIO). You won't find a lot of flights from the European hubs to and from Bilbao. You may have to fly back to Madrid. However, as discussed in my chapter on this subject, consider going directly to Bilbao when you arrive in Madrid or Barcelona. All you need do is transfer over to the domestic side of the MAD or BCN airport and fly up to Bilbao for about $100, plus of course, your bags. You will probably have to clear customs, retrieve your bags and recheck them into your domestic flight to Bilbao. It would be best if you allowed at least a four-hour window for that connecting flight, since you will have to walk over to the domestic terminal in BCN or take the shuttle at MAD.

MORE ON OPEN JAWS AND STOP-OVERS

If you are booking any "open jaws," you will need to book them under the feature called "Multiple Cities" as they do not state "open jaw." This is different from a round-trip ticket. Also, consider contacting the airline directly and see if they will allow a one-way stop-over. This is usually allowed from their hub-cities. For example, you may be able to spend several days in Amsterdam before continuing to Madrid or Barcelona at no additional cost as long as you are buying a round-trip ticket, e.g., **JFK-AMS-MAD-AMS-JFK**. Usually, they only allow one stop-over, inbound or outbound.

SCOTTSCHEAPFLIGHTS.COM

Now, if you are flexible, here's what I do. Subscribe to a website called *scottscheapflights.com*. It's only $39 a year and worth more than gold! Did it ever occur to you that airlines sometimes make mistakes setting up fares? So, say the usual fare from New York to Madrid on Iberia for March and April is $589. Mistakes happen, and the computer sets it up for $389. Scott's Cheap Flights notices this because it is so out of line with other published fares. They immediately send an email and inform you which airline has the fare and the travel dates. Repeat; all they do is notify you! You must still go to Iberia's website and book the trip directly.

In addition to mistake fares, there are also low ball "tickler" fares which usually come out when they publish the eleven month (330 days) forward schedule.

Remember, you must still book the fare yourself directly on the airline's website or use another website like Google Flights or Momondo. All these fares are usually non-refundable, and most airline policies may include one bag, in addition to meal service. There may be a nominal fee for a reserved seat. Else if you check-in at the counter, you will be given any available seat at no charge. Despite these small, sometimes extras fees, the fare is still a bargain. So, if you have the flexibility, Scott's Cheap Flights is the answer.

What you need to do is subscribe to Scotts. You only get about 20% of the deals over the website, so you need the $39 service to get notified immediately. You must also act immediately. So if you are seriously planning on "railing" through Spain, you must JUMP at a low ball fare and book it immediately. Yes, immediately! That's right, drop everything and do it. If you don't, those fares will probably not be available tomorrow. A fare of less than $500 round trip to Spain is a steal.

On my suggested Two Capitals Tour (Barcelona and Madrid), I recommend a ten-day minimum. Anything short of 10 days will be a real push. You can always add extra days here and there unless you already purchased your return flight. **READ THIS ENTIRE BOOK FIRST!** Remember, since most flights are overnight, you will need at least one full day to recover from no sleep and jet lag. Forget that first day when you arrive. All you will want to do is drop yourself in a bed and go to sleep! So plan your first trip with this book. When that rock bottom fare (8-10 months out) comes up on Scotts, book it immediately.

>>>TIP<<<
Again, I would strongly suggest that you read this entire book and then make your airline reservations or wait for Scott's email. Once ticketed, it is extremely costly to change a reservation. Think about it. It will cost you at least $1000 (with a rock-bottom fare) for a

couple to fly to Spain and perhaps only $300 (hotels and meals) more to extend it another two days. It is always better to spend a few more days than a few less. Best to look for the low fares in the off-months.
>>>>><<<<<

RESERVATIONS & MORE RESERVATIONS

The chapters and itineraries in this book follow a format. First, I try to provide a rough out of a day-by-day journey for each itinerary. Don't feel you have to follow it just that way. If you want to add an extra day here and there, go ahead and do it. Before you book any hotels and trains, make sure you have "fixed" your itinerary. Many low fares on the Spanish trains are non-refundable, just like the airlines. The same goes with certain hotel booking engines (OTA), e.g., *hotels.com*, *booking*.com, *expedia*.com, etc., which offer you a lower cost for a hotel room in exchange for a non-refundable rate. This is another reason I always favor dealing directly with a hotel rather than using a booking engine. Also, best to have all your hotel reservations before you go. Imagine arriving in Cordoba, only to find out that every hotel room is gone because of a "congress" (convention) in town.

CHAPTER 5

RAIL ITINERARIES OVERVIEW

INTRODUCTION

This book makes it easy to see Spain without an escorted tour which is often quite pricey and highly disciplined. I modeled these tours after our fully escorted tours of Spain and Portugal. You can spend one, two, three or four weeks in this historically rich and beautiful country which I enjoy second only to Italy. Or, should I say equal to Italy. If you follow my itineraries, you'll be assured of a most enjoyable and nearly stress-free visit.

My rail tours of Spain are basically broken down in to how much time you have available to visit Spain. Couple this with your prior experience (if you have visited Spain before), and you will find several of my rail tours just right for you.

I have devoted a chapter to each itinerary. Here is a quick summary:

CHAPTER 6:
BARCELONA AND MADRID ITINERARIES
7-10 DAYS, TWO WEEKS WOULD BE BETTER

If you have never been to either city and perhaps this is probably your first trip, consider visiting just these two cities. If you can only spend one week, this is ideal. I discuss both of them in Chapter 6. If you have been to Barcelona because you may have originated on a Mediterranean cruise, consider starting with my Itinerary "C." This begins in Madrid then goes south to Cordoba, Granada, and Seville. This region of Spain is known as Andalusia. It includes these historic cities as well as the Costa del Sol (CDS), The Sun Coast.

>>>TIP<<<

Suppose you are planning a Mediterranean (Med) cruise in the near future. In that case, you should realize that many of the one-week cruises originate in Barcelona, and therefore, you may want to save a visit to Barcelona till that Med cruise. Many of the cruises that originate from Rome (the port city of Civitavecchia) also pay a one or two-day visit to Barcelona. One-week cruises out of Barcelona usually are quite in-expensive (starting at about $700 for the week) and afford you a few days of sightseeing in Barcelona before the cruise begins or ends. Also, if you are originating in Rome or Venice, most cruises offer shore excursions when they arrive in Barcelona.

Many cruises also terminate in Barcelona, offering you the opportunity to take the train to Madrid and visit the historic cities outlined in my day trips out of Madrid after a two or three-day stay in Barcelona.
>>>>><<<<<

Barcelona and Madrid offer excellent day trips which are easily reached in about an hour from the city.

CHAPTER 7: BARCELONA DAY TRIPS

While in Barcelona, I have included one free day. My suggestion is to add another day so you can visit both Montserrat and Girona. Both are UNESCO World Heritage Sites and are easily reached via a one-hour train journey from Barcelona. Montserrat, about one hour west of Barcelona, is a monastery complex on the top of a mountain with breathtaking views. Girona is on the way to Perpignan, France, being about one-hour northeast of Barcelona. Girona is a walled city dating back to Roman times and is full of history, great for lunch and excellent shopping.

If you fly into Madrid and start your tour here, you will find that there are no free days in Barcelona for the two recommended day trips. My suggestion is either to eliminate one day from the Madrid day trips (definitely not Toledo) or add two days to the Barcelona visit. Let's face it; you have traveled a long way to get here; you may not be back, your grandchildren will be fine, so go ahead and spend a few extra bucks and add those two additional days!

CHAPTER 8: THE MADRID DAY TRIPS
In addition to sightseeing in Madrid, I offer three day trips: Medieval Toledo; Avila; Segovia with its monster Roman Aqueduct; and El Escorial, the Versailles of Spain. Except for Avila, all are reachable within an hour by train from Madrid. Avila, depending on the train, makes the run in 90 minutes to two hours.

CHAPTER 9: ANDAULSIA
CORDOBA, GRANADA AND SEVILLE
If you have a second week, head south to the land knowns as Andalusia (south of the "Plain of Spain"). This area south of Madrid is steeped in history, most of it going back to 218BC when Hannibal of New Carthage Spain (Iberia then) lead his army and elephants over the Pyrenees' mountains to conquer the Romans in what is now known as Italy.

The Moors first occupied the land of the Iberian Peninsula. Later came the Arabs from North Africa after crossing the Mediterranean. They settled in the places which were to become Cordoba, Granada, and Seville. All three cities are UNESCO World Heritage Sites, having numerous UNESCO historical monuments and or ruins. The three most famous are the Mezquita of Cordoba, the Alhambra of Granada and the Alcazar of Seville.

CHAPTER 10: MALAGA, MARBELLA, AND THE COSTA DEL SOL

After completing your second week, ending in Seville, consider the third week on the Costa del Sol (CDS). The CDS is part of Andalusia and spans the Mediterranean coastal area between the two anchor cities of Malaga on the east and Marbella on the west. There are two cities outside of the anchors which also are considered the Costa del Sol. They are Nerja to the east, famous for its underground caves and Estepona to the west.

Malaga and up the hills, Antequera contain UNESCO World Heritage Sites to see, and no visit to Malaga is complete without a visit to the Picasso Museum. Malaga and Antequera are easily reached by train.

From Malaga going west, the cities line up with resorts dotting the Mediterranean. Most of them are reached by railway (The C1 Cercanias train) from Malaga. These cities include Torremolinos, Benalmadena, Fuengirola, and a host of other smaller resort cities and towns. Marbella will be part of the C1 Cercanias line in the next 2-3 years. Two towns of historical interest are the hilltop towns of Mijas (best for dinner) and Ronda. I discuss Ronda as a day trip from Seville and the Costa Del Sol area. You should also consider Ronda as an overnight stop to the CDS area if you are coming from Seville. You will be halfway there.

The Costa del Sol area is where you want to be after touring Madrid, Cordoba, Granada, and Seville. Nothing beats lying on the beach for a week, especially if it's a spring or autumn week!

CHAPTER 11: SEVILLE AND THE COSTA DEL SOL DAY TRIPS: GIBRALTAR, RONDA, AND TANGIER MOROCCO

Ronda, Gibraltar (a British Colony), and Tangier, Morocco, are discussed in detail. It is difficult to get there by train; however, I provide the reader with coach (bus) alternatives and the use of "BlaBlaCar". BlaBla is the equivalent to "Lyft" and "Uber" in the USA.

CHAPTER 12: THE NORTH, BILBAO, SAN SABASTIAN, AND SANTIAGO DE COMPOSTELA

This region, known as the Basque Country, and the northwest corner above Portugal, known as Galicia, are a different area of Spain. It's the "North" of Spain, and you will probably visit it on your second and or third trip to Spain. You can certainly combine it with Barcelona and Madrid but unless you have a month to visit Spain, consider it a subsequent trip.

The number one draw to this region is, of course, the Guggenheim Museum in Bilbao. It's not the museum, it's the building. If you are of the Catholic persuasion, the other draw to this region is the Cathedral of St. James in Santiago de Compostela. You will need a day in each; and a day to transit from Bilbao to Santiago as they are on the opposite sides of this "north area".

CHAPTER 13: THE XYZ TOUR

The XYZ tour is what I would call a "whistle-stop or whirlwind" rail tour. It's modeled after that movie of many years ago called "If it's Tuesday, This Must Be Belgium". No side trips, only the major one or two highlights of each city. Just pack your carry-on bag and go. I can assure you that you will need a vacation when you get back home.

CHAPTER 14: LISBON…YES IT'S PORTUGAL

If you want to combine Spain with a visit to Portugal and the Lisbon area, I discuss it in detail. However, the best way is to fly it from Madrid in 90 minutes. However, if you insist, read the chapter for the details on the "Trenhotel". This was the overnight train to Lisbon. If you can't afford the Orient Express, this is the next best thing. While the Trenhotel is not operational now, provide you with alternate rail/bus.

CHAPTER 14: THE FRENCH CONNECTION

A few years ago, Renfe, the dominant rail operator of Spain, joined with SNCF, the dominant rail operator of France, to form "Elipsos", also known as Renfe-SNCF.

Since Spain now had high-speed rail service north of Barcelona into Perpignan, France, technically, the Spanish AVE train could run directly into Paris and other points in Europe. Great idea. However, this concept had to be marketed, i.e. seeing Paris and Madrid or Barcelona in one week. What a great idea. Because of the COVID-19 pandemic and some downturn in the tourism economy in Europe, there is only service from Spain to France and no through service to any other points in Europe. See the chapter for further details, times, and costs for this service.

>>>TIP<<<
I like to construct my itineraries such that I don't waste an entire day traveling from one place to another. My suggestion is to either take a morning train at about 9 or 10 AM or take an early evening train, i.e. a "sunset train." Both time frames allow you to view the terrain.
>>>>><<<<<

Since I do not know what chapters you have already read, I sometimes re-iterate specific points.

All my itineraries start with a "Rough Out." However, you don't have to follow that rough out the way I describe it. You can, of course, add a day here or there. However, be aware that some changes may have consequences. This is true especially for museums which usually are closed on Mondays. Also, street fairs which are very popular in Spain, occur only on certain days of the week. If you have your heart set on the Saturday street fair in Marbella, you must consider changes in your itinerary to accommodate this. It is best to check this out before swapping days.

On a final point in this chapter, read all the details about the Spain Eurail pass before you book any "long haul" train tickets. You may be able to save some money. Also, do consider the discounts for Seniors.

>>>TIP<<<
Here's a tip which really doesn't fit into any chapter, but I will share it with you. I learned it many years ago when I grew up in New York and traveled on the Long Island Railroad. Always try to face the direction of travel. You get to see what's coming up and when you turn your head toward the window you get to see it again. If you are facing the rear of the train, you only get to see out that window once. In addition, it's easier on your body if you are facing the direction of travel.
>>>>><<<<<

CHAPTER 6

BARCELONA – MADRID IN NINE DAYS

ITINERARY "A" (PREFERRED)

If you are planning the future a Mediterranean (Med) cruise, you should realize that many of the one-week cruises originate in Barcelona. Therefore, you may want to save a visit to Barcelona till that Med cruise. Many of the cruises that originate from Rome (the port city of Civitavecchia) also pay a one or two-day visit to Barcelona. One-week cruises out of Barcelona usually are quite in-expensive (starting at about $700 for the week) and afford you a few days of sightseeing in Barcelona before the cruise begins. If you are originating in Rome, most cruises offer an in-expensive shore excursion when they arrive in Barcelona.

Many cruises also terminate in Barcelona, offering you the opportunity to take the train to Madrid and visit the historic cities outlined in my day trips out of Madrid after a two or three-day stay in Barcelona.

I state that this is the "PREFERRED" tour because I assume that you may not want to take a Med cruise. To take in Madrid and Barcelona, it's best to start in Barcelona and then, if time permits, continue your travels to more of Spain which all emanate (because of the rail system) from Madrid. If you have seen Barcelona best, start your trip in Madrid under "ITINERARY B." If you have been to the City itself, consider another visit to Barcelona to see Montserrat and Girona. So here we go.

BARCELONA – MADRID

The Barcelona-Madrid rail tour of 9 days (including your fly days) is your introductory tour. You can extend it to 11 days if you add the two extra day trips in the Barcelona area: Montserrat and Girona. It starts in Barcelona then goes on to Madrid with three days of side trips: Toledo, El Escorial, Segovia, and Avila; all reachable by fast rail within 90 minutes. Barcelona's trip to Madrid takes two hours forty minutes on the high-speed Renfe AVE or the new SNCF TGV OUIGO train. The tour ends in Madrid, where you transfer to Madrid's Barajas airport for your flight back to North America or continue with Itinerary "C," Andalusia: Cordoba, Granada, and Seville. Here is your rough out of the rail tour:

ROUGH OUT:
Day 1- We fly overnight to Barcelona
Day 2- Rail Renfe airport train/METRO
   to your hotel (or taxi) then recovery;
   Las Ramblas, the old City,
   Montserrat or Girona (on Day 3 or
   Additional days in Barcelona).
Day 3- A day of leisure in Barcelona
   Perhaps the Picasso Museum?
Day 4- Morning AVE train to Madrid with a
   a visit to the Prado in the late afternoon
Day 5- Visit the Palace and City Tour
Day 6- Day trip to medieval Toledo
Day 7- Day trip to El Escorial
Day 8- Day trip to Segovia
   Optional extra day in Avila
Day 9- Fly home from Madrid's Barajas Airport

OVERVIEW- THE BARCELONA SEGMENT

Barcelona is broken down into the City itself and the two optional day trips, which will add two full days to your itinerary. They are Montserrat and Girona.

Barcelona sites not to be missed are:
A stroll on the Las Ramblas;
The Old City – right off Las Ramblas;
The Picasso Museum in the Old City;
The cathedral in the Old City;
The Gaudi houses – off the Plaza de Catalunya;

The central market on Las Ramblas.
The Plaza de Catalunya and Corte de English

And if you have time: The Museum of Modern Art a few blocks off the Las Ramblas. If you are into Gaudi, there is a Gaudi House Museum in the Park Guell.

Author's side note: If you add a day for Montserrat and a day for Girona, it will make this an 11 day trip instead of the nine days above. The best is to plan to go to Montserrat first and then to Girona on your second full-day trip. There is a lot of walking in Girona, and by this day, you should be recovered from that overnight flight and the jet lag.

OVERVIEW- THE MADRID SEGMENT

Itinerary "B" is about the same as itinerary "A" above. Except you fly into Madrid instead of Barcelona. You recover from your overnight flight in Madrid instead of Barcelona. Note, the train to Madrid from Barcelona is in the morning, and the train to Barcelona from Madrid is in the evening.

Like Barcelona, Madrid is split into the City itself with sightseeing at the Plaza Mayor, the Palace, the old market, and a visit to The Prado. The Prado is the equivalent of the Louvre in Paris. There are additional day trips that are included in my basic itinerary. They are Medieval Toledo (not to be missed), El Escorial (the equivalent of the Palace of Versailles (outside of Paris), Segovia, and the walled City of Avila. All of these are reachable by train in 60-90 minutes.

You will find a detailed ROUGH OUT of each day if you ORIGINATE YOUR TRIP IN MADRID, instead of Barcelona.

>>>TIP<<<
If you are planning on more to do in Spain, i.e., Seville, Granada, Cordoba, etc., you MUST start your itinerary in Barcelona, then go to Madrid where you will find trains to all points in Spain. There are limited trains out of Barcelona which bypass Madrid. However, most trains will force you to go back to Madrid and connect with another train for other points in Spain. However, there are a few AVE trains to Seville, but you would need to skip other cities as it skirts around Madrid over a new track built about 15 years ago. In summary, it is best is to originate in Barcelona, then go to Madrid, then go elsewhere in Spain.
>>>>><<<<<

ORIGINATING IN BARCELONA VIA AIR

This section describes your arrival in Barcelona from a flight from the USA, Canada, or elsewhere. If you arrive from Madrid on the train, skip this section and read the section "ARRIVING IN BARCELONA VIA TRAIN."

You can fly into Barcelona on most US major carriers, i.e., Delta, American, etc. All pretty much offer non-stop overnight service. You should avoid a connection or an overnight stay in London if at all possible, because of the higher airline British Government imposed taxes. These taxes are buried in the airline charges. However, if you are using Frequent Flyer miles, be prepared for British taxes. It is best to consult all the details in Chapter 4, "First Let's Get to Spain."

Other carriers such as Lufthansa, Air France, TAP, and Alitalia, to name a few, offer one-stop or connecting service directly via their European hub cities. Pretty much all of the flights are overnight from North America. Some of the hubs are Munich, Frankfurt, Paris, Lisbon, and Rome.

>>>TIP<<<
You want to arrive in Barcelona (airport code is BCN) between 6 AM and Noon. If you don't, by the time you get to your hotel and check-in, you will have lost a day of sightseeing. Also, note if you are only going to be in Barcelona and make the two Barcelona day trips, best if you can pack all in one of those "rollie" carry-ons.
>>>>><<<<<

>>>TIP<<<
I have always felt that the best places to stay in Barcelona are right off the Ramblas or the Plaza d

Catalunya. Avoid staying in the financial district. Also, remember that the BCN airport is eight miles south of the Las Ramblas area. So don't try to use your "hotel points" at one of the airport hotels. You will waste lots of time getting to and from the main attractions.
>>>>><<<<<

Once you arrive at BCN (airport code for Barcelona), there are two ways to get to your hotel. The Barcelona Metro system (their subway) does not come out to the BCN airport. Like Amsterdam and so many other European cities, it is served by a rail link. Renfe, the national railway system operator, operates a train about every 30 minutes into the City. It does not run at night! The train originates from terminal T2. If your flight arrives at terminal T1, you need to take the free shuttle bus over to Terminal T2. Most all flights from the USA arrive at Terminal T1. However, if you have heavy bags to carry instead of a "rollie" carry-on bag, it can be a hassle. However, you will find plenty of those storage racks for your large bags on the airport train.

If you are relatively young, i.e., not a senior, or are on a tight budget, consider taking the rail system. The Renfe train makes only three stops in the City: Sants Station, Passeig de Gracia, and Clot. You can change for the Green Subway line (the Metro), which will take you to the Las Ramblas area at Passeig de Gracia. Also, there are three stops on the Metro which runs under Las Ramblas. The Las Ramblas boulevard runs for about a half-mile from the Plaza d Cataluna to the Columbus monument at the harbor area. If you are using the rail system to get to your hotel off the Ramblas, you need to purchase for about 2.5 Euros a T-Casual one-day ticket. This ticket will allow you one hour and fifteen minutes of travel on the airport Renfe and the Green Line Metro (or any Metro train). Note, you should check the hours of operation of the Renfe airport train and the **METRO** since, as of this writing, they do not operate late at night. If you are making a connection in one of the European hubs, then connecting to Barcelona, you may arrive after 11 PM and be forced to take a taxi. All taxis operate at night but may have a surcharge and a baggage charge at night.

I do not recommend purchasing a multi-day Metro ticket if staying near the Ramblas area since all of the sites are right on or off the Ramblas.

If taking the day trip to Montserrat or Girona, you can purchase a Metro one ride ticket for the day to get over to Sants Station or the Plaza de Espanya (to get the train to Montserrat).

Also, AVE trains arriving at Sants allow you to use the Metro for one hour and fifteen minutes after your arrival. So no need to purchase a Metro ticket, if you have purchased a Renfe rail ticket.

>>>TIP<<<

It is best to ask your hotel in an email which Metro stop is the closest to their hotel to minimize walking: Catalunya (Plaza d Catalunya) or one of the other two stops on the Green Line, "Liceu" or "Drassanes." Also, some hotels are close to the Renfe airport train stopping at Passeig de Gracia and Clot stations, so there is no need to change to the Metro. All you need do is exit at one of these stations and walk a few blocks to your hotel.
>>>>><<<<<

>>>SUPER TIP<<<

I know this book is about taking the train instead of an escorted tour, but I have to say this. Consider that you have been flying overnight, you are bushed, you are a senior, and you deserve it!!! Take a taxi to your hotel on the Ramblas. It will cost you only 30 Euros and will be money well spent. You will arrive at your hotel in about 25 minutes. And by the way, taxi drivers in all of Spain do not expect a tip! However, as an American, I always tell the driver to keep the change, usually a Euro or less in coins. He or she will appreciate it.
>>>>><<<<<

There are several other ways to get to your hotel on or near the Ramblas. They all involve either airport buses or shared mini-vans. I don't know about you, but after flying all night and getting about two hours of sleep, the last thing I want to do is jump in a mini-van with other smelly tourists and make 5-7 stops en-route to my hotel, all to save twenty Euros. That will be twenty fewer Euros I will have to leave my kids. I'll enjoy it.

I might note there is one bus from the airport, which is known as the Aerobus www.aerobusbcn.com. It goes from BCN airport directly to the Plaza D Cataluna. It runs about every 15 minutes from Terminal T1 and only cost about six Euros. The only problem here is that you will still have to make your way over to T1, and you will have to lug your bags to your hotel on the Rambla. All I say is get me to my hotel, and give me a bed!

ARRIVING IN BARCELONA BY TRAIN

If you arrived on Day 7 of Itinerary B (see below) from Madrid on the high-speed AVE train and visited Avila during the day, you probably will arrive in the evening about 8–10 PM. If you care not to visit Avila, you can gain more site seeing time in Barcelona by taking a morning train from Madrid. Also, note you will not need recovery time. Figure you can arrive about the noon hour and head for your hotel on the Ramblas.

On arrival at Sants Station, follow the signs to taxis. It will cost you less than 10 Euros from Sants to your hotel on or near the Ramblas.

You want to stay on the Rambla or just off of it. Why? That's where all of the sites are. If you are in this corridor, you are only minutes away from all. And all of them are within walking distance. No need to take any tram, taxi, or Metro train. Avoid the urge to stay in one of those American-type hotels somewhere else in the City. Now here are your hotels whether you arrive via air or from Madrid on the train:

HOTELS ON, OR NEAR LAS RAMBLAS
I have included a list of more than twenty hotels either on or a few blocks off the Las Ramblas. Don't think to stay on the Ramblas the price of a room will be sky-high. It's not! There are lots of hotels on the Ramblas with all different prices; consult the Appendix.

There are probably over 100 hotels on or within a few blocks of the Ramblas. However, I must admit that my favorite is the Hotel Continental Barcelona at 138 Ramblas. The Continental overlooks the Ramblas (don't worry, the windows are soundproof when you close them) and is less than 200 feet from the Plaza d Catalunya. You should note that there is also another hotel called Hotel Continental Palacete. The Palacete is a little further up from the Hotel Continental Barcelona located on the other side of the Plaza d Catalunya. If you are taking that Renfe train from the airport, you will find that this hotel (the Palacete) is less than 100 feet from the Passeig de Gracia train (not the

Metro stop) station. So there is no need to take any Metro train. Just make sure you don't have any big clumsy bags to cart up and down the stairs or escalators….it's a drag (no pun intended)!

I always favor (except for London and Paris) taking a taxi or a private car from the airport. You can find private cars with drivers on the internet and for a few Euros more, will meet you with a sign with your name on it, lug your bags and take you right to your hotel. And remember, make your booking for your private car and your hotel directly! Also important is to put away those hotel points and stay at a European-style hotel. It's part of the total experience of travel. Hey, I can stay at a Hampton Inn in the good old USA, anytime.

And remember, on arrival at the hotel, you will have to surrender your passport. Don't worry. They will give it back to you when you check out. And don't worry, European hotels usually never asked for a credit card on arrival. It's Gauche (coming from the word Gaudi). It seems there is more trust here than in the USA. You will receive a bill when you check out.

Okay, so we have now checked into your hotel on or near the Las Rambla. So now, what do we do next?

If you have just arrived from that overnight flight to Barcelona and your hotel can accommodate you, the best is to take a one or two-hour power nap and then take a shower and get ready to get on European time. Avoid sleeping through the night. My first time to Madrid in 1972, I did this, overslept and woke up at 4 AM, and missed an entire day. The best is to call the front desk and have them give you a wake-up call.

>>>TIP<<<
If you arrive in the morning, email the hotel a week before you leave and ask them to accommodate you at about 9 AM. Do ask for a quiet room.
>>>>><<<<<

So change into something casual (consult the chapter on Security, Cash, Credit Cards, telephone calling, etc. and exit the hotel for the local sites. Remember to turn in that big key if your hotel has not converted yet to "key cards," else it will tear a hole in your pocket.

THE BARCELONA HIGHLIGHTS

My suggestion on that Day 2 free day or the arrival day from Madrid, by train of course, is to stroll the Ramblas:

If you walk down the Ramblas toward the harbor (statue of Columbus), you will want to make several stops. The first stop should be the large food market, known as the Mercado de La Boqueria (on your right), then swing into the Old City (The Gothic Quarter) and visit the cathedral and walk the cobblestone curved streets. You will find the Old City right across the Ramblas. You should also realize that with most in-town markets, many stalls start closing down about 3 PM. So don't count on that stall selling dried fruits and nuts to be open when you walk back Ramblas at 5 PM.

There are many cafes where you can enjoy a snack and a cup of American Coffee. You will find lots of them in the Old City abutting the cathedral. Lots of shopping in the area also. I might note, now is the time to select a place to have dinner. Do check out the restaurants and make a reservation for 8 PM.

Did you know that the Old City is home to the largest Picasso Museum in the world? It is housed in several medieval buildings and contains more than 4,000 works of the famous 20th Century artist. You can purchase tickets online at museupicasso.bcn.cat/en/.

>>>TIP<<<
If you can spare several hours and plan your Barcelona visit before you arrive, you will find no charge to visit the Picasso museum on Thursdays. Further, after 4 PM on many days, there is also no charge. You may find that the best time to visit the museum is first thing in the morning since you may be bushed from doing all that walking late in the day. Best to consult the website if there are any changes to the gratis days and hours, else you will have to pay about $15 for the general

admission. If you go to the Costa Del Sol area, you will also find a much smaller Picasso museum in Malaga.
>>>>><<<<<

If you are a serious shopper or have forgotten something for your trip, you will find it at the Plaza de Catalunya. Here you will find Spain's department store, known as the Corte de English, Primark (an excellent discount clothing store out of London) and other fine shops. You will find the Plaza de Catalunya at the beginning of the Ramblas, as the Columbus monument is at the end at the harbor side.

Several blocks from the Place de Catalunya are some of the famous Gaudi Houses. These buildings were designed by the Spanish architect Antonio Gaudi in the early part of the 20th Century. You cannot miss them! If it looks like something odd, it is probably one of the three Gaudi houses in Barcelona. There are tours offered of all three houses. In Barcelona, there is also a Gaudi Museum. Of the three famous buildings, my favorite is the Casa Batllo. When I saw it in the distance, I knew it was a Gaudi House. There is also a cathedral in Barcelona designed by Gaudi. The buildings were constructed between 1880-1920.

>>>TIP<<<
When walking the Ramblas, the Old City, the market, or the Plaza de Catalunya, watch out for pickpockets.

There are many scams. Please consult the chapter on this subject at the rear of this book. Be extra cautious when viewing what I call "those human statutes." You will know them when you see them. Feel free to drop a few coins in the bucket and be extra careful when bending over!
>>>>><<<<<

There are just too many places to see in Barcelona on an afternoon. Another suggestion I have is to put yourself on a half-day orientation tour. On check-in at your hotel, consult the concierge. Many half-day tours leave about 2 PM or even 3 PM in the summer. You can also plan this tour for Day 3, which would be your full day in Barcelona.

>>>TIP<<<
If you book your Barcelona city tour through the concierge many times, they will insist on cash since they take their commission out of the proceeds. Best to book online or thru one of the information booths or directly at the tour office. In this case, they will take your finc credit cards. My personal feeling on this is not to take a city tour. Unlike Rome, London, and Paris, most of the sites are right off the Ramblas.
>>>>><<<<<

>>>TIP<<<
Make sure you buy some munching food in that market on the Ramblas. Remember, since you are in Spain, most restaurants don't open for dinner until 8, 9 or 10 PM. Who eats dinner at 10 PM anyway?
>>>>><<<<<

If you are going on to Madrid after your full-day (it's the day after you arrive in Barcelona), you will want to get a train 9–9:30 AM to Madrid. This allows you to visit the Prado (Spain's famous museum like the Louvre of Paris) after your arrival and check-in to your hotel.

If you have one extra day in Barcelona, I recommend the day trip to Montserrat, via rail, of course. If you have two days, consider the Medieval City of Girona, also only one hour away by train. These extra days I discuss in detail under a chapter that follows. If you did not add any extra days in Barcelona, you should be on:

Day 4- Morning AVE train to Madrid with a
    a visit to the Prado in the late afternoon

TAKING THE TRAIN TO MADRID
Do not, repeat, do not, plan on going to Madrid without a ticket and a reservation. You need to book and pay for your tickets before you leave the USA or Canada. The best is to book them thru Raileurope (raileurope.com). You will pay a small fee, but they will

send you the tickets with your reserved seat numbers, etc. Ticketing for most **Renfe AVE (high-speed trains)** is available four months in advance, but this does change. So, don't try to book six months out.

As of this writing, in May 2021, a 9 AM departure from Barcelona Sants to Madrid's Atocha ("Atocha" for short) takes about 2.5 hours and will cover a distance of 376 rail miles. It will cost you about $40.

You should note as tickets sell out and on holidays the price of the tickets goes up dramatically. If you wanted to take this same train on December 31, 2021, it would cost you about $150. Renfe uses the same pricing algorithms of the airlines, e.g., when the plane is 50% loaded, they increase the fares 30% and forty-eight hours before a flight, expect to pay double what it would have cost had you purchased it six weeks prior.

All seats on the train are reserved. So, you cannot afford to miss your train, else you will have to re-book and may have to wait several hours or the next day for the next train and an available seat, oy, oy, oy.

AVE trains to Madrid run every two hours from about 6 AM to 10 PM. As of this writing, there are no overnight trains. You should check online for the new Ouigo train schedule, which took effect in May, 2021.

Like most European trains, it usually doesn't cost much more to go First Class (Preferente Class). You get a more comfortable seat, sometimes a beverage, a newspaper, or a light meal, i.e., a bowl of soup and a sandwich or salad. In addition to first-class (Preferente Class), Renfe also offers Turista Plus, the equivalent of Preferente Class, however, with no meals. Of course, the basic fares are coach or second class as we call it and are called just plain Turista Class in Spain.

I always feel that it's a toss-up between First Class (Preferente) or coach Turista. Hey, you are on vacation. Spend the extra $$ and go first class on this train. Best as stated before, have Raileurope handle it all for you. It's worth that extra ten or so dollars!

Another point, do not attempt to fly between these two cities. Unless you are connecting from a flight from Mallorca or the Canary Islands (considered domestic flights since they are Spanish islands), it will cost more money and more time to fly between Barcelona and Madrid. Certainly not worth it! Let's face it why would you want to fly from New York City to Philadelphia? You can hop on the train in Penn Station and be in Philly in 90 minutes.

All AVE trains to Madrid depart Barcelona Sants station. It's not Saints, but Sants. The name Sants comes from the old section of the town where the station is. Best if you are staying near the Ramblas or the Place de Catalunya to have your hotel call a taxi. If it costs you eight dollars, it will be a lot. If you have just those small carry-on "rollies," the best is to hop the Metro. You should note that only three Metro lines have stops at Estacio de Sants. You may have to change lines. It would be best to spend five extra dollars and just taxi-over from your Las Ramblas hotel.

You should allow 45 minutes before departure to arrive at Sants. If you want to make a more leisurely trip and not get that morning train, you may have to skip the Prado. Do check closing times at the Prado. On arrival, you can always visit the Plaza Mayor and walk around Old Madrid. Best to save the Prado for the next day. Also, if traveling Preferente Class, consider checking into the Preferente Class (Sala Lounge) lounge and having a coffee and some pastries before your train departs. Relax, that's what it's all about.

Once you arrive at Sants and are not traveling Preferente Class (where you get a meal), it's best to get that sandwich to go. Plenty of places at Sants to get some food to go (Take-away), and don't forget that liter of water. Prices are usually quite reasonable. However, you can also pick up something to eat within a block or two of your hotel. Remember that if you are going via Preferente Class (truly first class), you will enjoy a meal and a glass of wine.

Unlike Madrid's Atocha Station, Sants is a modern underground station. On arrival at Sants, ask any of the Renfe people where the AVE trains for Madrid depart. Certain platforms are specifically for Cercanias or in Catalan "Rodalies" (commuter trains). Then walk to the section where the AVE trains depart for Madrid.

In the large waiting room, keep your eyes on the electronic departure boards. When your train posts for boarding, head for the "VIA" (track number in Spanish). The posting usually occurs about 20 minutes before departure. You will need to go through security with your bags and carry-ons. Don't forget to take your food and water with your carry-ons.

Once past security, you will see several trainmen (ticket inspectors). Feel free to show them your ticket, and they will point you to the proper carriage. If you are running late, feel free to hop on any coach or carriage (marked **COCHE**) and "walk the train with your bags" until you are in the correct carriage. Then find your seat (your **PLAZA**) and stash your bags on the racks or behind your seat.

If you are traveling with a companion (spouse, friend, or whatever), make sure they watch your personal items if you go to the club car or the toilet. If traveling single, make sure you take that laptop or purse with you. Yes, to the bathroom! I usually have another couple or someone else watch it. You just don't know these days who is walking the train and picking up stuff!!

So sit back and relax, turn on your laptop, take a snooze and enjoy the Spanish countryside. It's a mix of farmland and hills. Nothing breathtaking to see, so just relax. In about two and a half hours you'll arrive at Atocha station in Madrid.

>>>TIP<<<
If you have a reserved seat on the right side of the train (going forward), you will see Montserrat (described in the chapter on the Barcelona Day Trips) in about 20 minutes after you leave Sants station. Best once again, when you make the booking, do ask the Raileurope person since they would know the layout and seat numbers on the AVE train. I believe you want to be on the right-hand side (looking forward).
>>>>><<<<<

ARRIVAL IN MADRID ON THE RENFE AVE TRAIN FROM BARCELONA

Continue here if you are arriving into Madrid on the train from Barcelona. If you are flying into Madrid, consult the section heading **"ITINERARY B ORIGINATING YOUR TRIP IN MADRID"** below.

If you have taken my suggestions, you will arrive at Madrid's Atocha station 12 Noon-1 PM. Great.

Atocha is split into two sections. The AVE and other high-speed trains are in the newer section. In contrast, the commuter (Cercanias) trains and other regionals are under an old train shed with a beautiful atrium. It's a unique station in that you will feel like you are in a greenhouse. Trust me; you will know the difference between the two sections.

Your AVE train will arrive in the new section. From here, you will have to make your way to the older area where the regionals and the Cercanias trains depart. Atocha is like an airport! You need to follow the crowd (they are only going one place) up those "Travelators" (we call them escalators) onto the footbridge across the tracks to the ARRIVALS EXIT. Following the crowd will take you to the old trainshed, which now looks like an arboretum with almost 300 species of trees and bushes. The place is quite impressive, with several dozen eateries and shops.

If you have not had any nourishment or just snacks on the train, consider having a sandwich or salad at Atocha station before making your way to your hotel.

Now you need to check in to your hotel. If your room is not ready, you will check your bags in the bag room. I usually don't suggest checking your bags in one of the lockers at the rail stations unless you are returning this way later in the day. I certainly would not check my bags here overnight. If you have to check them overnight, best is the bag room in your Madrid hotel.

I have suggested three great day trips from Madrid in this itinerary, all within 40-90 minutes away. Since you may have added two days in Barcelona for Montserrat and Girona, those day trips in Madrid are Toledo, El Escorial/Segovia, and Avila.

Since all three sites are readily accessible by rail, my suggestion is to be within walking distance from Atocha or no more than a five-minute taxi ride. If you are staying at any other hotel in Madrid, you can take the Metro from Atocha. Bear in mind that you may have to transfer from one line to another to reach your hotel. Take it from me; it will be a hassle.

The best is to walk to your hotel or take a taxi for less than $10. Line 1 is the only Metro line that serves Atocha. Also, note that Atocha has two stops on Metro Line 1. The station marked "Atocha Renfe" is the closest to the "Atocha Station" while "Atocha" is closer to the Reine Sofia Museum.

>>>TIP<<<
Suppose you are taking the Metro from Atocha to another hotel, not in the Atocha/Prado area. In that case, you can use your AVE ticket for one hour and fifteen minutes of travel in Madrid after you arrive from

Barcelona. Don't throw that AVE ticket away; you will have to scan it to enter the Metro platform.
>>>>><<<<<

Other popular hotels, outside of the Prado/Atocha area are located on the "Gran Via" or near the Plaza de Espana. Staying in a hotel on or off the Gran Via is like staying in New York's Times Square. It's pretty noisy with buses and cars honking, not to mention the papers blowing in the street and the chaos of all those tourists moving around. I feel it's a turnoff for Madrid. Don't compare this with quaint Old Madrid, which is a 10-minute walk from the Gran Via.

There are numerous hotels in the Atocha area that are within walking distance. What I mean by walking distance is that they are no more than a 10-minute walk. Hotels in this category I list in Appendix B. It would be unfair to recommend any of these hotels since I have never stayed in them. It's best to read the reviews on Tripadvisor and Booking.com. If the Poor plus the Terrible category in the Tripadvisor reviews exceeds 20% of the total reviews, I usually will not stay there.

Within a taxi ride of less than $10, you will find many hotels. Remember to take those day trips; you will have to either walk back to Atocha or take a taxi. You probably want to take a cab on your return, since you will probably be exhausted from all that walking!

>>>TIP<<<

While I have stayed over the years in many hotels in Madrid, my favorite has always been the Hotel Puerta de Toledo. It's located on the square of the same name. I love it for many reasons. First, it's just a 10-minute walk into Old Madrid, the markets, the squares, the shopping, etc. On the weekends, it's a few blocks from a major street fair, and thirdly, there are several cafés around the entrance to the hotel where you can purchase anything from a full dinner to just a snack, coffee, and a great dessert before you retire for the evening. Also, you will find a drug store just across the street. It is located in an upscale residential neighborhood. If you are of the Catholic persuasion, you will find the Basilica of San Francisco el Grande just a few blocks away. It's about a mile from Atocha and will take you about 21 minutes to walk it. The hotel's location is just fine for day trips, but I prefer to hop in a taxi if I had my big "rollie" bag.
>>>>><<<<<

If your budget does not allow taxi fares of $20 a day, your best bet is to camp yourself out at one of the hotels in my table of no more than a ten-minute walk from Atocha. It would be best if you also considered the Prado Museum location with respect to your hotel. After you drop your bags at your hotel, all you need do is walk a few blocks over to the Prado.

So we are now in Madrid; what do we do?

OVERVIEW OF MADRID

Of all the European cities I have visited, Madrid is undoubtedly one of the youngest. Don't look for ancient ruins or Roman or Greek temples. You won't find them. Some ruins date back to the time the Moors occupied the Iberian Peninsula. However, Madrid dates to about 1550. The old name was actually "Mayrit." Think of it. That's only about 60 years after Columbus discovered America. No, Columbus did not ask Queen Isabella in Madrid permission to find the "new world." He asked Queen Isabella in Cordoba. Madrid probably was a small hamlet then.

I have always seen Madrid as a modern city compared with Rome, Paris, Jerusalem, and Athens.

Here are the must-visits:

THE PRADO-

Madrid is right up there in being home to one of the leading museums in the world. If you have heard of the Louvre of Paris (home of the Mona Lisa), this is next in line. Take it from me. I have been to the Rijksmuseum in Amsterdam, the British Museum in London, the Uffizi in Florence, and a list of other fine museums. The Prado tops them all! I cannot say enough about the Prado. Why? Well, for a starter, it houses the most extensive collection of Renaissance Spanish artists (and others) in the world. Just think of it? Where can you find so many Goyas, Rubens, Velazquez, El Grecos, and more under one roof? The Prado celebrated its 200th birthday in 2019. Of all the paintings in The Prado, the most famous is the *Las Meninas* by Velazquez. Before you go to the Prado, you should read up on it in Wikipedia. You must reserve a ticket to the Prado before going to Spain. Like the Uffizi in Florence, do not expect to show up at the Prado and request a ticket. Many times they may be sold out.

I might note that there are three other museums worth a visit if you have time. Consider visiting two other leading museums of the world. They are the Thyssen-Bornemisza and the Reina Sofia. They are located only a few blocks from the Prado. And consider having lunch, at the Museum of Ham (no kidding). The Museum of Ham is also known as "Museo del Jamon". The Ham Museum is a few blocks from the Prado at Calle de Alcala, #155. Here is a short overview of Reina Sofia and the Thyssen-Bornemisza.

The Reina Sofia houses incredible works of Picasso, Dali, and Miro, all Spanish artists of the 20th Century.

At the Thyssen-Bornemisza, you will find works from the 13th Century to the 20th Century. They include Rubens, Monet, Van Gogh, Gauguin, Klee, Hopper, to name a few. There are over 1000 paintings. Both museums are worth a visit if you are a museum lover.

>>>SUPER TIP<<<

Consider going to The Prado in the evening before or after dinner. It's free. However, you must get a ticket online before you leave for Spain. The sooner, the better. This is a bargain, considering dinner at 8 PM >>>>><<<<<

>>>TIP<<<

Once you enter the Prado from the street, you will see licensed docents wearing badges in the foyer. These docents will explain the significant works of art to you—no need to rent those audio headsets. The docents will escort you through The Prado for about 25-40 Euros for a group of up to four. It takes about 60-90 minutes. Most of them only accept cash, no credit cards. Do consider haggling over the price. Always hold the money in your hand seems to work all the time, as in "show me the money." This is money well spent. I won't steal their thunder; however, when the docent takes out that small mirror when you view the *Las Meninas* and says, "take a look at this," it will send chills down your spine!

Suggest you make sure the docent speaks English quite well; if you are not satisfied, best to "interview" another

docent. Just be diplomatic. It's okay. Just a note, the younger docents will speak English.
>>>>><<<<<

THE ROYAL PALACE

The Royal Palace is another "must." It comes in at about half the size of the Palace of Versailles at 1,450,000 square feet. It's up there with all those other palaces of Europe, i.e., Schoenbrunn in Vienna, the Winter Palace in St. Petersburg, Russia, etc. It is the largest functional palace in all of Europe. I might note that Buckingham Palace is about half the size.

There are 3,418 rooms in this monster palace. It's the size of one of those mega-hotels in Las Vegas. But you can't stay here. Sorry. The Palace is the official residence of the royal family of Spain. However, no one stays there. The Palace dates from the year 860AD when the Moors of Cordoba controlled it. The original construction was started by Muhammad I of Cordoba.

Tickets usually are 6.50-13.00 Euros depending on the path thru the Palace. It is best to purchase them online at the official website of the Government of Spain: https://entradas.patrimonionacional.es/es-GB/informacion-recinto/6/palacio-real-de-madrid

You should note that on some dates and times, there is no charge. However, expect to wait in line to get into the Palace. You can walk over from the Plaza de Espana, but it's easier just to take the Metro to the "Opera" stop and walk about two blocks.

INTRODUCTION TO OLD MADRID

You will love Old Madrid. It's one of my favorite places in all of Spain. If you plan this right, you can visit all three sites as I describe them below: Mercado San Miguel, The Plaza Mayor, and the Casa Botin. They are all within a few blocks of each other. If you are pressed for time, the best way to visit all three is to go about 5 PM to the Mercado. Then visit the abutting shops in the area. When you are pooped, pick out a nice place on the Plaza Mayor for a drink and some tapas. You will be lucky if they have that Spanish hot chocolate on the café menu. It has the consistency of liquid chocolate pudding; else, try the Spanish beer. If you are with a group of one or two other couples, go for a selection of tapas and wash them down with a pitcher of Sangria; save the dessert for that hot chocolate.

Then about 7:30 PM, walk over a few blocks to the Casa Botin for dinner. I often skipped dessert at the Botin (flan doesn't do it for me) and had some ice cream (better Gelato) at the Plaza Mayor. Anyway, hopefully, you can spend more time in and around Plaza Mayor. I might note that if you are staying at the Hotel Puerta de Toledo, you will certainly enjoy the walk into Old Madrid as there are numerous shops and markets. By the time 10–11 PM comes along, I can tell you that I only have enough energy to hop into a taxi for a five-minute ride to Hotel Puerto de Toledo. So here we go:

THE PLAZA MAYOR

Dating back to the 15th Century, Plaza Mayor was the central market for Madrid. The main square of the Plaza now functions as a multi-function venue. Everything from flea markets and bullfights to soccer games has taken place at the Plaza Mayor. If you want to mingle with many people in a crowded square, this is the place. It seems everyone turns out at the Plaza Mayor from 9 PM. Just remember to watch out for those pickpockets and scammers.

Around the buildings of the Plaza you will find lots of restaurants, cafes, and shops. If you have a second night in Madrid, this is the place to have dinner. Else, best you should have dinner at the Casa Botin, the oldest restaurant in the world.

DINNER AT THE CASA BOTIN

A few blocks off the Plaza de Mayor and down the street from the Mercado San Miguel, you will find the oldest restaurant still in existence, The Casa Botin. Rumor has it that it had its origin in the year 1590. Its official name is Sobrino de Botin. However, locals and tourists refer to it as Casa Botin or just Botin. It's not dinner here; it's the experience. Supposedly, Goya worked here as a waiter (when he wasn't painting), and Hemingway bussed tables here when he wasn't fighting in the Spanish civil war. Their specialty is Segovian (from the town of Segovia about 50 miles north of Madrid) roast suckling pig. Two can share the portion. I have had it several times, and I can tell you it does not taste like a pig or any ham, but more like veal. It is oven-roasted, and I give it a "10". Their prices are not expensive at all. Botin is a must if you are visiting Madrid. It's only a 20 minute walk from the Prado area or the Hotel Puerta de Toledo. Best is a taxi for about six Euros, or better stroll the four blocks after visiting the Plaza Mayor.

>>>TIP<<<
If you intend to experience dinner one night at the Casa Botin, you must make a reservation about 45 days before your arrival in Madrid. Do ask for a cozy table in the "cellar" or basement. If the staff has time, they will give you a five-minute tour of the kitchen after dinner. You can find out more about the Casa Botin on their website: "https://www.botin.es/en/home/. And remember, dinner usually starts at 8 PM. Also, men leave the suits and sport jackets home, and ladies forget those high heels. With heels on it is difficult to walk down that circular staircase to the cellar (lower level). If you are visiting outside the summer months, best to take a sweater. Casa Botin is laid back!
>>>>><<<<<

MERCADO SAN MIGUEL

The "Mercado" was the market of Madrid and dates to 1916. San Miguel was renovated and re-opened in 2009. If you grew up in New York City, it's like going to the Old Washington Market on Greenwich Street in lower Manhattan, which disappeared when they built the World Trade Towers in 1973. However, unlike the Washington Market, it only has about 30 stalls. The place is dramatically lit up at night with glass walls. You will know it when you see it. If you want to take some pastries back to your hotel for an after-dinner treat, this is the place where you will find them.

PUERTA DEL SOL

Like Times Square is to New York City, Puerta Del Sol is to Madrid and Spain. "Sol" is the place where the eating of the grapes takes place on New Year's Eve. "Sol" is also the "Zero" point where all the roads radiate to other parts of Spain. Lots of shops on the abutting streets. It's worth a day's visit. However, I have never found any real shopping deals in Madrid. Save your shopping for Ronda and the street market at Marbella, both in the Andalusia and Costa del Sol area.

THE GRAN VIA

No question, this is the Broadway of Madrid. However, you won't find any theatres here like you would find in New York, London and Toronto. However, there are several movie theatres—just a lot of hotels, shops, money exchanges, and architecturally interesting buildings. The Gran Via (Great Way) has been "renovated" several times since its early 1900 creation. Most recently, a pedestrian walkway has been created. This place is worth a stroll for about a half-mile up to the Plaza Espana.

EL RASTO FLEA MARKET

This flea market is a monster! Very similar to the monster one in Paris at Porte de Clignancourt. Don't compare El Rasto to Portobello Road in London. You probably could drop 30 Portobello roads into El Rasto. It's only open on Sundays and what is known as "Bank Holidays." Over 3,500 vendors are hawking practically everything. The flea market dates back over 400 years. It's an easy walk from Puerta de Toledo and most of those hotels in the Atocha/Prado area. It is located in the La Latina area, and you can spot it on the map at La Ribera de Curtidores and the cross streets.

There are numerous cafés and fast food eateries at the market. The most important thing to remember is that this is a haven for pickpockets. Best to read my chapter in the rear of this book on security, etc.

SUMMARY OF MADRID
Most critical places you must visit:
 The Prado
 Old Madrid- Plaza Mayor, Mercado San Miguel

   Puerta del Sol
   Dinner at the Casa Botin
If you have more time:
   The Royal Palace
    A walk on the Gran Via
    El Rasto Flea Market (Sunday's only)
    In the evening a Falmenco show or if you are going on to Seville, see it there.

If you are starting your Spain visit in Madrid and flying into Barajas Airport (MAD) you should continue with Itinerary B. Below:

ITINERARY "B"

MADRID-BARCELONA

ORIGINATING YOUR TRIP IN MADRID

This section describes your itinerary with an overnight flight from North America to Madrid (MAD) and a departure at the end of the week from Barcelona.

ROUGH OUT:
Day 1- We fly overnight to Madrid
Day 2- Rail (the Metro) or a taxi to our hotel
     near Atocha, Recovery day, The Prado
Day 3- Leisure day Madrid

Day 4-   Visit the Palace and City Tour
Day 5-   Day trip to medieval Toledo
Day 6-   Day trip to El Escorial
Day 7-   Day trip to Segovia evening train to Barcelona
             Or an optional extra day in Avila
Day 8-   Barcelona city tour and leisure time
Day 9-   Fly home from Barcelona or day trip
             to Girona or Montserrat

OTHER PLACES TO ORIGINATE A SPAIN VISIT: With the exception of a combination visit of Spain and Portugal, all vacations (holidays) will usually begin in Madrid or Barcelona. These cities, as stated before, offer direct non-stop flights to and from the US. You can, of course, add Lisbon to these cities. Many folks who have the liberty to take three weeks of holidays can fly to Lisbon and then take the train to Madrid (see chapter on this subject) and continue with the other itineraries. I have devoted several pages to this under the chapter entitled "Lisbon…Yes, it's Portugal".

You can also originate your trip in many of the "minor" cities: Seville, Malaga, Cordoba, Granada, etc. However, these cities are only reached via European connections, i.e., Paris, Frankfurt, Munich, Amsterdam, etc. So as of now, don't expect to fly non-stop from JFK to Seville!

GETTING FROM THE BARAJAS (MAD) AIRPORT TO MADRID CENTRO

It's Day 2, and you have just arrived at Madrid's Barajas Airport. Welcome to Spain! The airport is located 12km northeast of central Madrid. If you figure the center of Madrid is the Puerta del Sol, then the airport is at 2 PM. You have been flying all night, and you are entirely "wrong out." I know the feeling, having done it many times. Here are your options:

THE METRO FROM BARAJAS AIRPORT (MAD)

The subway system does come out to Barajas Airport and makes two stops. They are terminals 1, 2, and 3, the new terminal a mile away is referred to as T4. Terminal 4 is where most overseas flights depart and arrive. You can't catch a flight here to the Canary Islands as they usually depart from the old airport terminals 1, 2, and 3. For about $5, the Metro Line 8 (PINK LINE) will take you to Madrid, making several stops. It only runs one way from the airport, i.e., directly into Madrid. Unfortunately, you will probably have to connect to another line or perhaps two other lines before reaching the closest Metro stop to your hotel. It runs every 8 minutes.

The Metro system of Madrid is quite complex. It is very much like Paris and London, and totally unlike New York. I mean to say that all the lines crisscross each other and do not run in straight lines like the subways of New York. If you are going to your hotel in the Atocha area or the Hotel Puerta de Toledo, you need to plan your trip on Metro Line 8 (their subway) before boarding the train. You should know your stop.

Instead of taking the Metro (Subway), take a look at the next section, which is faster and more convenient than the Metro, where you must change trains. It is known as the Renfe C1 LINE.

RENFE TRAIN TO MADRID ATOCHA AND SEVERAL OTHER POINTS (THE C1 LINE)

This was constructed several years ago and is part of the RENFE commuter network knowns as Cercanias. This train goes into Madrid and makes several stops, the first one being the "other" large train station of Madrid known as Chamartin. It also costs about three Euros and runs every eight minutes and takes about 20 minutes to get into the City. The nice thing about this train is that it goes to Atocha, which is the fifth stop. Make sure you don't fall asleep on the train, or you will pass Atocha and wind up at the last stop, which is "Principe Pio." This new commuter line (C1 Cercanias) cuts across the City (very similar to the RER of Paris) and makes other important stops. If you are not staying at the Atocha/Prado area, you can usually get off the train and walk to your hotel. Using the C1 train allows you to walk directly to your hotel in the Atocha/Prado area, else take a taxi for about five Euros to the Hotel Puerta de Toledo at the plaza by the same name. The C1 line only runs from the new TERMINAL 4 (T4), so you must take the courtesy shuttle from T1, T2, or T3 over to T4. As discussed, if you are flying in from North America, you will arrive in T4. If you have connected somewhere in Europe, i.e., Amsterdam, Paris, etc., you probably will arrive at T1, T2, or T3.

There is one other alternative, and that is the express bus to Atocha. It costs five Euros, runs every 15 minutes and takes about 40 minutes to reach Atocha. You can figure another 15 minutes if there is heavy traffic. You cannot miss this bus (Exprés Aeropuerto) as it is bright yellow. It does not stop at Terminal 3. However, you are in luck with a host of empty seats and nothing on the baggage racks as it originates at Terminal 4. The bus will take your popular credit cards. You should note, it does make two or three stops before reaching Atocha. If you are staying at a hotel, not in the Atocha area, you may be able to get off the bus closer to your hotel.

However, if you are bushed and want to spend the extra bucks, take a taxi directly to your hotel. It will cost you about 30 Euros (about $35). And of course, if you want to spend the big bucks, you can be taken in style to your hotel by a private driver. Nice thing: they will meet and greet you with a card with your name on it, lug your bags, and tell you about Madrid. It's worth another $30 over the taxi fare. Having a private car and driver meet you and escort you to your hotel is excellent if you are a party of four people. Best deal going!

COMPLETION OF MADRID-BARCELONA SEGMENT IN MADRID

If you have completed your 7-10 Madrid Barcelona segment, at this point, you have several options:

1. Continue south to Cordoba, Granada, and Seville on Itinerary "C" See Chapter 9 -or-
2. Go north to Bilbao and San Sebastian (The Basque Country) "E" See Chapter 12
3. Continue your rail journey to Lisbon on the night train. Or take a one hour flight.

If you are going on to the south of Spain, known as Andalusia, and terminating your rail trip in Seville, it is best to fly out of Seville. You will not find any non-stop flights, so you will have to connect via one of the European hubs or fly back to Madrid and connect there for your flight back home.

If you are considering a third week in Spain and visiting the Costa del Sol area, also reachable by train, you will need to fly out of Malaga (AGP). Once again, you will need to fly out to one of the European hubs or connect in Madrid or Barcelona for your flight back home.

This concludes my Barcelona and Madrid rail Itinerary. Now visit the chapters on the Barcelona and Madrid day trips.

BALANCE OF THIS PAGE LEFT BLANK FOR YOUR NOTES-

CHAPTER 7

BARCELONA DAY TRIPS MONTSERRAT & GIRONA

INTRODUCTION

After you have enjoyed the highlights of Barcelona and you can spare a day or two, there are two day trips worth their while. Montserrat is by far my choice. It is a mountain top town located about 30km northwest of Barcelona. A one-hour train ride easily reaches the town. The other, located about an hour northeast of Barcelona, is the historic town of Girona. This is also reached by train from the city center. Before going on, I must inform the reader that Montserrat and Girona do require a whole day. You can figure arriving about 11 AM and departing about 5-6 PM. It would be best if you figured lunch in this time frame. If you only have one extra day in Barcelona, my choice would be Montserrat.

MONTSERRAT:

About 30 miles northwest of Barcelona lies a mountain range known as the Montserrat mountains. It gets its name from Mont for mountain and Serrat for jagged. Think of a serrated knife or the sharp teeth of a saw.

The highest peak of the range is a little over 4,000 feet. The mountains are composed of numerous outcroppings of gigantic boulders and other types of rock formations. The scenery is breathtaking.

The most important site of this mountain range is a monastery on one of the mountains known as Montserrat. The monastery was erected in the 11th Century. There are several other chapels, a large convent, shops, and a museum. What is most important is that Montserrat is the home of the Black Virgin Mary with the child Jesus on her lap. It's a long story, so best to read up in one of the excellent tour guides on Barcelona. If you are of the Catholic persuasion, you can also attend Mass at the Basilica. Check the times on your arrival at the plaza.

The Benedictine Abbey and the Monastery of Montserrat can be reached by car, bus, and train. However, the best way is the R5 train and the cable cars or the rack railway. An escorted tour bus or car to the top of the "mont" via the auto road does not compete with the breathtaking views of the rack (Cremallerea of Montserrat) or the cable cars (the Aeri) to the top.

>>>>TIP<<<
Visiting Montserrat will require an entire day. Under no circumstances "short" the day. There is too much to see and do, and you will need time to take the train up

the mountain (it's a rack railway, sometimes called a COG railway in the USA) and then back down. Or you can take the cable car up and down, or any combination of rack and cable car. You will need to be on the train from Espanya Estacion in Barcelona about 9-10 AM. It would be best if you planned on leaving Montserrat and heading back to Barcelona at about 5 PM.
>>>>><<<<

Now here is how to do it:
You need to take either METRO line L1 or L3 (the Red or Green line) to the Espanya Estacion (just called Espanya metro station). If you are located near the Las Ramblas area, you can also walk over. It would be best if you allowed about 30 minutes to walk over to the METRO station. Once at the METRO station, you will have to take the R5 FGC train. This is not a METRO (subway) train, but a commuter train, very similar to the RER in Paris. No need to worry about which direction since the R5 FGC train originates at Espanya Estacion.

Now here is what you need to know. There are two stops on the R5 line that will take you to Montserrat (the village at the base of the Montserrat mountains). If you plan to take the cable car to the top, you need to exit the R5 train at "Montserrat Aeri," which is the first stop. There is no real town around the cable car station. It's just a cable car station (with restrooms). If you plan on taking the special train to the top of the mountain (The

Rack or Cremallera, not the cable cars), you need to get off the R5 train at Monistrol de Montserrat, which is the second stop on the R5 line in Montserrat. The Cremallera is located in the town of Monistrol.

On exiting the R5 at either station, no need to follow signs or ask directions; just follow the crowd. They are all going to the cable cars or rack railway.

>>>TIP<<<
If you are taking the cable cars to the top, it is best to ride in the last car on the R5 train. When you exit the station, you will be first in line for the cable car loading.
>>>>>><<<<<

>>>TIP<<<
I suggest you take the rack train up the mountain and the cable car down the mountain. Why? Simple, the cable cars run every 15 minutes and allows you to get that next train back to Espanya station in Barcelona on the R5 line. If you take the rack train back, you will need to allow more time since the rack trains run back down the mountain every hour.
>>>>><<<<<

>>>TIP<<<
If you have mobility issues, you need to take the rack train each way. There are some minor steps to climb after you exit the cable car landing on the top of the

mountain. The cable car does not support wheelchairs.
>>>>><<<<<

>>>TIP<<<
The price of a ticket on either the cable car or the rack train is less than ten Euros. However, at the Espanya station, you can buy a combination ticket which includes the R5 train ride, and travel up and down the mountain on the rack. You can also buy a combination ticket that includes the R5 train and then up and down the cable cars. However, no ticket allows up on the cable cars and down on the rack or vice-versa. So if you decide to go up on the rack and come down on the cable cars (suggested), you will need to buy a one-way cable car ticket on the plaza abutting the Abbey. Make sure you arrive early enough at the Espanya station to purchase your tickets. You do not want to run for that R5 train!! There is usually an "FGC" assistant to answer questions. FGC is the short name for the regional railroads of Cataluna, officially known as Ferrocarrils de la Generalitat de Catalunya.
>>>>><<<<<

I suggest that you go over to Espanya station and check out all the combination tickets a day or two before you want to go. There is an FGC person there who speaks English and will assist you. You also can purchase a round-trip ticket only to and from Montserrat. Then go to the rack railway stop on the R5 (Monistrol, the

second stop), take the rack train up, and then take the cable car down. As discussed, you will have to buy a one-way ticket down the mountain on the cable car.
>>>>TIP<<<

The best approach is to purchase just the R5 ticket in combination with either the rack railway up the mountain or the cable cars. Many people complain that the 50 Euro package includes just too much to see in a day, i.e., the museum, the Saint John and Santa Cova funiculars, lunch, etc. So best to purchase at Espanya station the basic package as just mentioned. You can also find more information on the current tickets, combos, and pricing on the large yellow machines operated by FGC (the operator of the R5 train). Those large yellow machines are clearly marked "TRAIN AND RACK" or "TRAIN AND CABLE CARS." The ticket booth and machines will take your credit cards.
>>>>><<<<<

>>>TIP<<<
Having lunch at Montserrat is very expensive. There are picnic tables on the terrace area abutting the Mirador dels Apostols, and also great views. It is best to ask your hotel concierge where you can have some sandwiches made up for your journey. There are also many in and around Espanya station. Trust me on this one! And don't forget a liter of water!
>>>>><<<<<

As a final point, if you care not to take the R5 Line and the cable car or the rack railway to the top of Montserrat, there are many half-day and full-day tours. You should bear in mind that most of them take the motorway to the top of the mountain. There are two problems here. One, the escorted tours are pricy, and two, you don't get to take the cable car to the top or the rack railway, which is in my opinion 80% of the experience of going to Montserrat for the day.

If you want further information, the government of Catalunya has a website devoted to getting to and from Montserrat. If you wish to, consider purchasing your tickets online instead of stressing out once you get there: www. cremallerademontserrat.cat/en/home/

And one more thing, nothing beats planning. It is best to know what time your return train departs and allow lots of time to get to either station in Montserrat. Enjoy your visit to Montserrat; else you will enjoy dinner and spend the evening in a hotel in the village of Monistrol; not a bad idea. Enjoy an evening with the locals.

>>>TIP<<<
If you are taking the cable car up the mountain, you want to be first in line and sit or stand at the rear of the cable car. In other words, not the view going up the mountain. On your return, when you are going down the mountain, you want to be first into the cable car and

face the downward direction. In this way, you will get the best photos without anyone being in your way.
>>>>><<<<<

>>>TIP<<<
The return ticket from Montserrat on the R5 is quite expensive. This is not a two Euro ticket. After the trainman inspects your ticket, put it away in your wallet or purse along with your passport!
>>>>><<<<<

MONTSERRAT RECAP:
Travel time from Espanya station to Montserrat Aeri or Monistrol d Montserrat is about 60 minutes. Total trip time connecting (from Barcelona) to the cable car or the rack railway to the top of the mountain (the monastery) is about 90 minutes.

The R5 Train operates every hour from Espanya.
The cable car operates every 15 minutes.
It is about 5 minutes to the top exit of the cable car.
The rack railway from Monistrol takes about 20 minutes to make it to the top.
The rack train operates every 30 minutes.
You should consult my hand-drawn map of Montserrat at the back of this book.

GIRONA

About 62 miles northeast of Barcelona lies the city of Girona. The city is divided between the new city and the old one, which is surrounded by the remnants of the old city walls dating to the Roman empire. The ancient Iberians, along with the Romans, the Moors, and Charlemagne, made their mark on Girona.

>>>TIP<<<

I would strongly suggest that you do a lot of reading on Girona. There is just too much here to see and do. Four to six hours is not enough. So my suggestion is to consider an overnight trip to Girona. You can do it two ways. Just leave your bags in your room in Barcelona and pack one overnight bag you will take to Girona. If you plan your Spain trip with a dedicated visit to Girona, you can check out of your room in Barcelona and leave the bags with the concierge, who will lock them in the baggage room. On your return from Girona, all you need do is retrieve those bags and check in again or, better that evening, head back to Sants and take the high-speed train to Madrid. Planning, Planning, Planning, there is no substitute for it.
>>>>><<<<<

As for hotels in Girona, my choices would be Hotel Historic, Pensio Bellmirall or the Cas Cundaro. You will feel you are staying in the old city. Most hotels, of course, include breakfast. And remember to email the hotel, book directly and ask for a quiet room.

Here is how you get there:
About 20 trains a day travel between Barcelona and Girona each way. If you want to take the fast high-speed AVE train, you need to book in advance (raileurope.com or Renfe.com). They make the run in about 40 minutes before going on to France. You must make a reservation either online or on arrival in Barcelona as all first and second-class seats are reserved. Make sure you book your return trip late in the day. If you have finished your touring in Girona at 5 PM and your return train is at 7 PM, you can always find some time to enjoy "nada" with a coffee and some tapas at a local cafe.

If you care not to spend $25 each way, you can take a slow regional train which takes about 90 minutes (sometimes two hours) and makes about 12-20 stops for about $13 each way. No reservation is needed; purchase your ticket at the station.

Most trains to Girona depart the central train station in Barcelona known as Sants, whether AVE, or other high-speed trains, or just plain old local trains as described.

>>>TIP<<<

You should note that there are several departures and returns from the two other stations in Barcelona. They are El Clot Arago and Sant Andreu Comtal. Best to check with your concierge the night before so you can plan your day. If you are staying near the Las Ramblas, you can hop the Metro with your T10 cards to Sants station. Allow at least 40 minutes to catch the Metro and buy your ticket once at Sants. Frankly, I'm into high-speed trains, so I would prefer the express reserved AVE train for about $25 each way—only a 38-minute ride. And don't waste your money on first class. By the time the train rolls and you go to the café car for a snack, you will arrive in Girona. Remember to get off; else you may wind up in Perpignan, France!
>>>>>><<<<<

It's best to depart Sants about 10-10 AM and return from Girona, leaving about 7 PM. You can "play" with the schedules favoring the 40 minute AVE type trains.

It would be best if you remembered that all AVE, TGV types, and other high-speed trains require you to be on board 5 minutes before departure. Also, you will need to go through a security check just like the airlines. It would be best if you figured arriving in Sants about 30 minutes before departure. There is no need to pack a lunch. Girona has numerous cafes and restaurants.

Now once you arrive at the Girona station, you immediately learn a little history about the place. Get this: The railroad arrived in the last 100 years; however, the town dates to about 700AD. In summary, the rail station lies about one kilometer outside the historic area. So you can figure about a 20-minute walk a little more than a half-mile to the center. Buses are available. However, you can pile four people into a taxi for five Euros. Best to use the taxi on the return when you are too exhausted to walk that half mile back to the station.

>>>TIP<<<
Since trains run every hour to Sants station in Barcelona, you should make a note of the return time and plan on being back at the Girona station at least 15 minutes before that train arrives from the north, else you will wait another hour! No problem, if you have purchased/reserved a seat on the AVE type trains.
>>>>><<<<<

Here is what to see and do:
You can walk the medieval walls, which date back to the Roman Empire. From the tops of the walls, you can take great pictures of the city. The walls are quite extensive, and there are still some towers remaining.

If you want an experience similar to Medieval Toledo (Madrid day trip), walk the streets in the old Jewish Quarter, which dates back to the 10th Century till the year 1492 when the Jews of Spain were asked to leave by Queen Isabella unless they converted to Catholicism. The Quarter is a maze of cobblestone streets. It is one of the best-preserved Jewish Quarters in the world. There is a Jewish Museum in the old Quarter. Check days of operation since the Museum may be closed on Saturday and other Jewish holidays.

Also, do check out the abutting Medieval town of Besalu. It's just a short walk of about six city blocks. Here you will find the Jewish Baths (Mikveh), and more of an ancient city ruled in the years after 878AD by "Wilfred the Hairy." Yes, you read it right. This rather odd ruler was a hairy guy!

One site not to miss is the Cathedral of Girona. It dates from about the year 1000—lots of steps here to climb.

If you are a fan of "Game of Thrones," you will realize that many scenes are filmed in Girona. Make sure you check out those beautiful colorful buildings on the five rivers. Wonderful pictures here! Finally, lots of shopping, small boutique hotels, cafes, and other eateries adorn this wonderful old medieval city.

GIRONA RECAP
You will need an entire day.
AVE type train takes about 40 mins, cost $25 each way
The slow train takes 90 minutes, cost $11 each way

AVE from Sants only. In other stations, the slow or Commuter trains from Sant Andreu and El Clot Arago. Consider spending the night in Girona.

CHAPTER 8

MADRID DAY TRIPS
TOLEDO
EL ESCORIAL
SEGOVIA
AVILA

INTRODUCTION

Whether you have started your trip in Madrid or arriving from Barcelona on the high-speed AVE train, you will enjoy these day trips in the Madrid area. If you need additional days, you can certainly add them to your planning a few months before you leave the USA.

If you have to prioritize these day trips, my recommendations are: Toledo, (pronounced tow-lay-dough) an absolute MUST. Next would be El Escorial and Segovia, followed by an entire day in the walled city of Avila. Here is a quick overview of each day.

TOLEDO

Toledo is one of the most famous walled medieval cities in the world. It is a UNESCO World Heritage Site. You can easily spend an entire day here—lots of shopping and many places to have lunch. The three most important sites visited are the Cathedral, The two Jewish Synagogues, and the Alcazar (fortress).

EL ESCORIAL

What the Palace of Versailles is to France, El Escorial is to Spain. It is massive, and to boot, the town of San Lorenzo (El Escorial) is packed with shopping.

SEGOGIVA

My next choice is a day trip to Segovia, home of the Alcazar of Segovia, which was adopted as the castle in Disneyland. Also, it contains one of the largest and best-preserved Roman aqueducts in western Europe.

AVILA

Outside of Toledo, my final choice for a day trip is to the walled city of Avila. I am sure you have never been to a medieval town with a wall like this. Would you believe people flock to Avila to see the wall?

Except Avila, all cities/towns are reached by train within one hour. It's a fast 90 minute run to Avila.

As discussed with the day trip to Girona out of Barcelona, you may want to overnight in Avila or Segovia. Further, it would be best to stay in the old city.

People ask me, "if I am going south to Toledo, why can't I go further on to Cordoba." The answer is quite simple: You must go back to Madrid Atocha and transfer. Toledo and Cordoba are on different rail lines.

Since your day trips may be limited, it is best to read all the details about them in travel books. Then make your decision before you leave for Spain.

DAY TRIP TO TOLEDO

Because of limited tourism in 2020 and further in 2021, Renfe has limited trains to and from Toledo. As of this writing, in May 2021, Renfe lists about six trains each way every day. Most of these trains are in the early morning and late evening. They are Cercanias (Commuter) trains which carry commuters to and from Madrid. There are limited trains during the mid-day.

>>>TIP<<<
Don't let the hotel concierge talk you into taking the bus for a few four Euros less. It will take you about an hour perhaps even more with traffic.
>>>>><<<<<

>>>TIP<<<
You may be interested in taking a full or half-day escorted tour. It's not a bad deal and will cost you about $50 per person. However, bear in mind that it is very regimented and you may not have the time you need for

shopping and lunch. Also check if the tour includes all admissions i.e. Cathedral, etc. Many of them do not! Suggest you read all the reviews before you book. Also, you will need time to get to the tour bus departure point as they may not pick you up at your hotel.
>>>>><<<<<

If you are going on the Toledo day trip, you need to get a train 10-11 AM from Atocha. The medium-speed train is an AVANT class which will take 32 minutes and cost you about 11 Euros. The train is double ended (like most AVE type trains), and makes Toledo the last stop before reversing direction and heading back to Atocha. Unless you are staying over, you need to take a train around 5-7 PM. The fare and and time will be the same.

All trains depart and arrive at the old trainshed known as Atocha Cercanias. Don't worry. It's the same Atocha we all know. Arrive early to get tickets. Then keep your eyes on the electronic departure board for the "Via" (track number). When your train number, destination, and time are posted on the large train board, proceed to the track, clear security and hop on the train. Walk the COCHE's until you find the correct coach and seats you reserved if taking a reserved seat train. Most of the trains which are un-reserved have only one class of seating. Yes, it's second class or better Tourista class; no problem, it's only a 30-minute run.

En route to Toledo, the train passes through Madrid's urban areas, industry, and then rolling farmland.

On arrival, follow the crowd to the awaiting bus or the taxis. All tourists are going the same way. If you are not a senior and physically fit, you will have to walk over to the bridge that spans the Tagus river and then walk up to the old city. Repeat-walking up that steep hill should not be attempted by seniors.

If you are a senior or have compromised mobility, take it from me, hop a taxi at the station and tell the driver to take you to the Alcazar. Else, you will puff your way up that hill to the old city. A taxi will cost you no more than 6-7 Euros for a carload.

Since Toledo is a walled city built on a hill, it is difficult to "get up there." However, once in the City you won't have to climb any hills. You should wear your sneakers as most of the narrow streets are all cobblestone type.

>>>SUPERTIP<<<
If you are on a tight budget or not use to huffing and puffing up a hill, you should board the local bus #5, 61, or 62 for 1.5 Euros, and it will take you to the central square in Toledo in about 10 minutes. Take your time picking up that information at the tourist booth. There is a bus every few minutes. Take note of the bus stop and bus number since you will probably board one of

these buses on your return to the rail station. Most of the bus drivers will speak some English.
>>>>><<<<<

There is also a Hop-On-Hop-Off bus. However, it doesn't do justice to the old city as it only spends 15 of the 40 minutes in the old city.

>>>TIP<<<
On arrival at the train station, stop off at the Tourist Information (TI) booth and pick up the maps, booklets, and discount coupons. Also, check the train schedule for your return trip to Madrid, else you will be forced to have dinner in Toledo and take the last train back to Madrid or better find a hotel to overnight in Toledo, which wouldn't be a bad idea.
>>>>><<<<<

By order of importance, here is what I suggest:

The Cathedral (Primada) of Toledo- if it's a really sunny day and you catch the light just right, you will be pretty impressed with the stained glass over the alter, 40 minutes here. There may be a small entrance fee.

The two ancient Synagogues of Toledo, located in the La Juderia quarter of the old city- Now turned into a museum but quite impressive. You will need 15 minutes to find the second one. I always get lost.

I just love walking the Old City with its stone walls (what's left of them), turrets, and all those cobblestone winding streets, thinking about my Spanish ancestors who walked the same streets prior to 1492.

Great shopping: There are four places in the world where you can purchase Damascene Jewelry. You will know these works of art when you see them. They are not a lot of money. Perhaps $50 for a pair of cufflinks or something small enough to stuff in a stocking for a Christmas gift. You will find almost a dozen shops with skilled artisans creating these works of art.

The Alcazar- The fortress now turned museum that appears in every picture of Toledo, only if time permits. Best to take photos of this place unless you are staying overnight and will have some time the next day.

About 5 PM (check the departure times for Madrid on arrival in Toledo), start to work your way back to the rail station, either taxi or take one of the buses (#5, 61, or 62). It's a fast 30-minute ride back to Atocha. Depart Atocha for your hotel and make sure you haven't left anything on that train. On arrival at your hotel, you should be able to enjoy a half-hour power nap and a nice cool shower, before dinner at about eight.

DAY TRIP TO EL ESCORIAL (Closed Mondays)

This day trip is one of my favorites. However, after the Toledo day trip, I would visit Segovia next, then El Escorial, and then Avila.

I have always combined El Escorial with a visit to the "Valley of the Fallen" (*El Valle de los Caidos*) just about five miles up the road. However, because of the COVID pandemic, it is temporarily closed. Once open, four people can hop in a taxi for about ten Euros or less and visit this basilica of black marble. This "basilica" is a bored tunnel the length of a football field. It is the home to over 30,000 soldiers who died on both sides of the Spanish Civil War. The basilica was also the resting place of the Spanish dictator Francisco Franco until October of 2019, when his remains were removed and taken to the family plot in a cemetery in Madrid. If you are on the C-3 train bound for El Escorial, take a look on the left-hand side in about 15 minutes out of Madrid, and you should be able to see the 500 foot cross on top of the mountain which houses the basilica.

El Escorial lies in a beautiful town at the foothills of the Sierra de Guadarrama mountains about 28 miles north of Madrid. The town's official name is San Lorenzo de El Escorial. It is also a UNESCO World Heritage Site. Here you will find shopping and places to have a light lunch after you visit the monastery (actually now a palace). El Escorial is more than a monastery. It's a

Roman Catholic Basilica, a royal palace, a museum (fantastic and well-preserved tapestries), a school, and more. The entrance fee is only six Euros, and you purchase them outside the Palace at that booth.

The complex was built starting in 1556AD under the direction of King Phillip II. Of all the rooms in the Palace, the one not to be missed is the crypt or burial vault. Here you will find the resting places of most of the kings and queens of Spain. The room overlooks those beautiful mountains. You should allow about one hour to visit the main rooms of El Escorial.

HOW TO GET TO EL ESCORIAL
Don't try to look on the Renfe.com website for trains to El Escorial. You will find only a few per day. The town of El Escorial de San Lorenzo is considered a suburb community of Madrid and is served by the C-3 Cercanias (commuter) rail line. Note: it is NOT the Metro Subway line, also known as C3. They are two different rapid transit rail lines! The logo of the Cercanias service is a red circle with a reversed "C" in it. The Metro or subway is a diamond with an "M".

The C-3 Cercanias line starts in the town of Aranjuez on the south side of Madrid (there is also another palace here) and heads north through Madrid. You can board the C-3 train at the following stations: Atocha, Plaza de Sol, Nuevos Ministerios, and Chamartin in the city. So if your hotel is closer to these stations, there is no need to hike back to Atocha. There are also a few Renfe trains a day from Atocha, which are not the C-3 train but make a stop at San Lorenzo before continuing on to Avila. You need to buy a ticket for El Escorial (the station) for 4 Euros from the machine located at each station entrance. All Metro, Renfe, and Cercanias stations will take your Mastercard or Visa. When on the rail platform, make sure you get on the train bound for El Escorial (it's the last stop on the C-3 line). Do not get on the train for Aranjuez. You will be going the wrong way! Trains run every 30-60 minutes. The journey takes about one hour from Chamartin and one hour 10 minutes from Atocha, with stops en route. Because of the COVID-19 pandemic, trains from Atocha may not be running. There is no need to pack a lunch as there are many eateries in this town.

Once you exit the rail station, there is a mile-long walk slightly uphill to the Palace and the town's main street. However, the "L1" bus meets the trains coming from Madrid and for 1.5 Euros you can hop the bus. I might note if you have a party of four, best to take a taxi for about five Euros to the Palace.

As for El Escorial, I will not steal all those details and will leave you to obtain them from those detailed travel books. I always tell people that you should allow at least an hour at the Palace. There is a lot of walking.

I find it best to get a 10-10:30 train from any of the Madrid stations. In other words, try to arrive at any of the stations at about 10 AM. On arrival, either enjoy the stroll to the town or else take that "L1" bus or a taxi. If you intend to visit Avila the same day as El Escorial, you should consider a train at about 9AM. This will definitely allow lunch in Avila.

While this book is about rail travel, there are buses that will take you to El Escorial. Frankly, I like "walking" the train and enjoying the traffic on the abutting highway, especially those tolls north of Madrid.

>>>TIP<<<
You can also combine El Escorial with a visit to Segovia and return to Madrid from Segovia. Segovia has the same level of train service El Escorial has. There are two ways to do this. Leaving El Escorial, if you take the C-3 train toward Madrid, you will have to change trains at Villalba de Guadarrama. Once you get to Villalba de Guadarrama, in about 12-15 minutes, you get that train (if it's on time) to Segovia. From here, it's about 45 minutes to Segovia. You should check the Renfe schedule for exact train times. The train connections are a hassle, and I don't recommend it. However, there is a bus (autobus) once or twice a day between the two towns—best way to do this. Check with tourist information (TI booth) when you arrive at El Escorial station as times and operators change. If you are with

5 or 6 people, you may be able to negotiate a fare of about 60 Euros or less (on Uber or BlaBla Car, etc.) or so for the taxi driver to take you over to Segovia. Other than that, my feeling is making Segovia its own day trip. You would do better at combining Avila with El Escorial in one day, which is quite simple to do. See my **SUPER TIP** below.
>>>>><<<<<

>>>SUPER TIP<<<
Get this… it just so happens that Avila is on the same Renfe rail line as El Escorial. This is not the C-3 Cercanias train but a Renfe high-speed train. The trip takes less than an hour from El Escorial and only costs about $10—what a deal. If you get to El Escorial when it opens and leave after two hours, you can take a train direct (no stops) to Avila and have lunch there. I might note there are excellent places to have lunch in Avila. I usually favor Avila for lunch over El Escorial. When you return, you must go direct to Madrid. The fare is about $16 and takes about 90 minutes. Check the Renfe.com website. Best to plan the train times and allow enough time to get your tickets.
>>>>><<<

DAY TRIP TO SEGOVIA
Segovia is a walled medieval city in the autonomous community of Castile and Leon. Like Toledo and El Escorial, it is a UNESCO World Heritage Site. It's also

the capital of the Province of Segovia. While the wall around the city wasn't constructed until the middle ages, it has its early beginnings, about 75AD.

Segovia offers three big attractions. First, there is the historic Roman Aqueduct. Yup, I've seen lots of aqueducts, but this one is the daddy of them all. It looks like they just built it last week. After decades of falling apart, the government of Castile and Leon, with help from American Express (yes, AMEX), restored the Aqueduct to the way it looked when the Romans built it. After you take all those photos of the Aqueduct you can tour one of the oldest castles in Europe, the Alcazar of Segovia. Couple this with a visit to one of the late Gothic style cathedrals in Europe, the Cathedral of Segovia, and you will have plenty to do for a full day. If you have more time in Spain, I would certainly consider spending two days in Segovia. Just pack your bags and check-in and out of your Madrid hotel.

HOW TO GET TO SEGOVIA
It easy to get to Segovia. There are about ten trains a day each way, and most of them are the high-speed Alvia or Avant trains which are very similar to the ultra-high-speed AVE trains. To give you an idea of the speed of the trains, they cover the distance from Madrid to Segovia (56 miles) in 32 minutes. That's about the same distance as Kenosha, Wisconsin, is to O'hare Airport, which is certainly a lot more than 32 minutes.

Trains depart about every hour. However, it's best to get the outbound train at about 9:30-10 AM. Trains only depart from Madrid's Chamartin station. So you need to allow extra time to get to Chamartin and find your train. Rather than taking the Metro (subway) if you are in the Atocha area, Cercanias trains connect Atocha and Chamartin and make a couple of stops. Since the Alvia and Avant trains may require seat selection, it is best to purchase your tickets online at Renfe.com. You can figure a 5-6 PM return to Madrid.

On a slight negative note, when Renfe created this high-speed line, they relocated the Segovia rail station to an industrial park (Hortoria) about eight kilometers (five miles) away from the center of town. The station is known as Segovia-Guiomar. The old station still remains in town. However, the Spaniard's are pretty smart. So they have a shuttle bus (bus #11) meet all the trains and charge only two Euros to take you to the center of the town where the Aqueduct is (Plaza de la Artillería). They also offer return service from the same drop-off point in Segovia. Consult the schedule on drop-off when the return trips are to the rail station in Hortoria (Segovia-Guiomar). By the way, the bus ride only takes about 15 minutes. A taxi will cost you seven Euros, and I am sure the taxi driver will fill you in on the latest happenings in town and about his brother's restaurant which serves the best Segovian roast pig this side of Madrid. If you are overnighting in Segovia, figure about one more Euro, and he will take you directly to your hotel and drag your bags into the lobby.

The best deal is that the train is only about 11 Euros each way if you avoid the rush hour trains in the morning and late in the afternoon, which are double the price. As of this writing, in May 2021, here are the suggested times from Renfe:

Chamartin Station   Madrid-to Segovia   10:15AM
32mins, 11.10 Euros
Segovia to Madrid Chamartin   6:22PM
32mins, 11.10 Euros
Remember to get those reserved seats if needed and do arrive 30 minutes before departure from Chamartin.

By the time you get to the cafe car to get a coffee, the train will be slowing up for Segovia!

THE ROMAN AQUEDUCT
Supposedly this double-decked all-stone Aqueduct was built about the year 100AD by the Romans. It spans one of the squares of Segovia. Only the upper portion carries water from the Rio(river) Frio about 10 miles to the city. The lower deck only supports the upper stonework with the water carrying trough. At its tallest point, the Aqueduct reaches a height of almost 100 feet above the city square. The length of the actual

aqueduct bridge is about two football fields or figure about 600 plus feet.

I won't steal all the thunder about the Aqueduct in this book. However, suppose you are into civil engineering or want more information on the Aqueduct. In that case, best is to visit the museum of the Segovia aqueduct, which is located in the old Segovia Mint Building. Yes, where they made coins.

I might note that the Aqueduct itself extends outside the city for about a mile before arriving at the square.

I always recommend having lunch in many inexpensive cafes in the Plaza de la Artillería abutting the Aqueduct. Don't buy any of those souvenirs yet, unless you want to carry them around all day. I say this because the next major site to visit is the Alcazar (the castle) of Segovia. Allow plenty of time to return to the aqueduct area for shopping and your shuttle bus (#11) departure back to the Renfe station.

THE ALCAZAR OF SEGOVIA

It's a little over a mile walk from the Aqueduct crossing the square to the entrance of the Alcazar. To the base of the Alcazar, it's only 20 minutes and about a mile. If you are up to it, you should figure about 30 minutes with the last ten huffing and puffing your way up to the entrance. I have never walked it and have always taken a taxi for less than five Euros directly to the entrance. No huffing and puffing here as the taxi will take you right up to the entrance of the castle. Best to do this in reverse. Go from the Aqueduct to the Alcazar and walk back to the Aqueduct with a stop at the Cathedral. It's all downhill; thank goodness!

A short history of the fortress: The original Alcazar dates from about the year 1120AD when it was only a Muslim fort built over Roman ruins. Over the years, the Alcazar was modified to function as a fort, parliament, prison, military school, and a palace, to name a few.

The Alcazar lies on a craggy hill at the confluence of two rivers. You need to pass through the old city to find the Alcazar. Supposedly, the Disneyland and Disneyworld castles were modeled after this Alcazar.

Unlike the typical palaces like Versailles, Buckingham, and Schoenbrunn, this fortress turned palace contains numerous "great" halls, all worth a visit. If you have ever been to a real castle, you will enjoy the Alcazar of Segovia. You will need at least two hours here.

Surprisingly, the entrance fee is only five Euros. Now, if you want to climb the tower, that's an additional three Euros. There are breathtaking views of the countryside and Segovia from the 156 steps to the top of the tower.

Sorry, there is no elevator. If you are a senior or not in great shape, it's not advisable to do the climb.

THE CATHEDRAL OF SEGOVIA

As stated prior, the Cathedral de Segovia is one of a few remaining Gothic-style cathedrals in Europe. You can't miss it as it is in the Plaza Mayor (of Segovia). Construction started in the 16th Century and, if you believe, it took 250 (1525-1768) years to build. It is located abutting the old Jewish Quarter. Of interest are the building itself and its collection of stained glass windows. There is an entrance fee of five Euros.

>>>TIP<<<

You can walk to the Cathedral from the Aqueduct square via the Old City and do some shopping. Since they are all lined up in a row, after the Cathedral you can then proceed to the Alcazar. The Calle Real is the main cobblestoned street which allows a nice stroll through the old city and the old Jewish Quarter. You will find restaurants, bars, and eateries on this street (almost like an alley). If you are stopping off at the Cathedral, you will find the Pasteleria Limon y Menta across the street. The "Menta" is a great place to enjoy a café, pastry, or the Segovian hot chocolate before you continue your walk over to the Alcazar or if you are walking back to the Aqueduct.
>>>>><<<<<

>>>SUPER TIP<<<

Now that you have read everything about Segovia, I offer you the best solution without having sore feet at the end of the day: On arrival at the train station, take a taxi to the entrance and ticket booth to the Alcazar. After the Alcazar, walk down the hill and find the Pasteleria Limon y Menta across the street from the Cathedral. Enjoy some pastries and a hot chocolate (incredible). Then visit the Cathedral of Segovia. Walk the streets of the old city, do some shopping and find your way to the Aqueduct.

You should be at the Aqueduct about 2 PM, enough time for more shopping and lunch. About 3-4 PM, continue your shopping and then take Bus #11 back to the train station (or a taxi) to meet your evening return train. Train times change dramatically from month to month. As of this writing, there was a train at 3 PM back to Madrid. However, the next train is more than 24 Euros. Best to plan your day trip to Segovia before leaving the USA, or better, a minimum of 30-45 days in advance to get the best fares.
>>>>><<<<<

OVER-NIGHTING IN SEGOVIA

There is a lot to do in Segovia besides the three major sites as outlined above. However, to enjoy this medieval city, it's best to overnight here and enjoy some

Segovian roasted pig in many restaurants in town. Here is a shortlist of hotels I would recommend:

Eurostars Plaza – one block from the aqueduct
Hotel Real Segovia- Old Town
Hotel Condes de Castilla – Old Town
Hotel Spa La Casa Mudejar- One block from Cathedral
Hotel Don Felipe- three block from Alcazar entrance
Hotel Candido-A little out of the way but a good find
Hotel San Antonio el Real- five blocks from Aqueduct
    In a quiet area
Hotel Enfanta Isabel- Old Town
The Parador of Segovia- It's a new Parador (not a converted castle, monastery, etc.) with great views. About one mile out of town. You would need to take a taxi to and from the city center. Best to email the Parador and see if they have a courtesy shuttle service to the town center.

DAY TRIP TO AVILA

Avila (pronounced, Ah-vee-lah) is a medieval walled city in the province by the same name. It is also located in the autonomous region known as Castile-Leon. It is also the region's provincial capital and happens to be the highest city in elevation in Spain.

GETTING TO AVILA

Trains to Avila depart from Madrid's Chamartin station and the smaller station known as Principe-Pio. There are only about four trains a day from Chamartin while the main feed to Avila is out of Principe-Pio. Here you will find a train every two hours. It's what they call an "MD" train, fast but used for moderate distances. You usually do not need assigned seats. However, best to check the Renfe.com website and make sure you specify Principe-Pio as your originating station. The fare is about ten Euros each way and takes about 90 minutes. You can also get limited trains which stop at El Escorial. See my Super Tip on visiting El Escorial first thing in the morning and then going further on to Avila from El Escorial.

Since the rail station is not in the old city, you need to take a taxi to the main gate or closest gate to the Plaza Mercado Chico. It will cost you about 3-4 Euros. You can also walk it in about 20 minutes. Just keep asking "Don-day-estah Plaza Mercado Chico." And just watch the way the person points or makes those hand gestures like they do in Italy. For seniors, you should take note that you need to walk up a slight hill. Best to hop in a taxi for 3-4 Euros. On the return, consider walking down the hill on that wide path with the city wall on your left toward the train station, or better find one of those other gates which are closer to the station.

I have been to Avila twice and have thoroughly enjoyed it. As Orson Wells once stated, "that if he had to live in another place.. it would be Avila". It tells you a lot about a town. It is a UNESCO World Heritage Site.

What I like most about Avila is the wall around this ancient city. Supposedly this is the number one draw, not the squares or the Cathedral or the fact that this is the city of Saint (Santa) Teresa, but the wall. It is unique. Not your average wall (lol). The original wall dates back to Roman times (about 5th Century BC), but the wall you see now was built about 1090AD, 500 years after Rome fell. What is most interesting about the wall is the statistics: 1.5 miles around, 80 towers, and ten gates. Talk about being impressive. You can walk on top of the wall for most of the way and note those towers and crenels (the notches in the wall).

If you enjoyed Toledo, you would love Avila. Make your first stop the Mercado Chico. It is also the main square of the town, and it is flanked at one end by the city hall. Best to enter the walled city through the large main gate known as **Puerta del Alcazar**; then find your way to the Mercado Chico, only a few blocks away. Yes, the "Chico" is a market that has been going on for at least 500 years. In and around the Mercado Chico you will find excellent restaurants for lunch.

After lunch stroll your way around the cobblestone streets in the old city and find your way to the Cathedral. The Cathedral of Avila dates from about

1100AD. You can't miss it. It's made of several types of colored granite. The Cathedral is half church and half fortress and is built into the walls of the city.

Other notable churches not to be missed are the Basilica de San Vicente and, of course, the Monastery of Santa Teresa de Jesus (on the plaza by the same name). If you plan on visiting Avila, you should read up on Saint Teresa and her life.

There is also a famous church tower (it's not the Cathedral) where storks hang out. Yes, you read right… storks. In Spanish it is cigüeñas pronounced "see-wayne-yah." Just ask any of the locals where the "see-wayne-yahs" are, and they will motion with their hands. If you are lucky, you will see several nests, in the church belfries, with the young ones in them. Rumor has it that these storks spend their winters here in Avila after flying non-stop from North Africa.

Before leaving Avila and working your way back to the train station, all downhill, I would strongly suggest that when passing a pastry shop (pastelerias), do pick up some "Yemas" (Yemas de Santa Teresa). They contain no white flour but do contain sugar. Remember, you won't be having dinner in Madrid till at least 8:30 PM.

If you want a great walking tour of this walled city, visit www.kevmrc.com/free-tour-avila-spain. Information and the maps are free. If you don't stop at any site long, it will take 90 minutes to do 1.5 miles around Avila.

>>>TIP<<<

Avila hosts about four festivals a year. Plan your trip before leaving home. If you want to go to Avila for the day, make sure you do not go on a festival day unless you want to attend the festival. If you are there on a festival day, it will be pretty crowded. It will also be a feast for "pickpockets; be on the lookout!
>>>>><<<<<

OVERNIGHTING IN AVILA…

You should note that I only include hotels and B&B's in the Old City. There are upscale modern American-type hotels outside the city walls. You will find small boutique hotels located within the city walls. If you stay overnight, make sure you take some pictures outside the Old City when the walls are all illuminated.

Here are the hotels:
Hotel Las Moradas
Palacio de los Delada
Hotel Puerta de la Santa
Exe Reine Isabel
Hotel Las Leyendas
Don Diego (Guest house)

El Canto Hotel
Las Cancelas
Hotel El Rasto
H2 Avila

As a final note, it is best to combine El Escorial in the morning and Avila, with lunch in the afternoon. Best to take a train about 7PM back to Madrid.

This chapter ends the Madrid day trip section. I do hope you enjoyed it.

CHAPTER 9

CORDOBA, GRANADA & SEVILLE

ITINERARY "C"

INTRODUCTION

Cordoba, Granada, and Seville are the most famous of the historical cities known as Andalusia. However, when people ask me about the region, I tell them about these three cities. There are many more minors, i.e. Antequera, Ronda, etc. These three leading cities are steeped in history. Over several thousand years, they have changed hands many times. First, some quick geography of the region.

Andalusia lies south of the Castile-La Mancha (Plain of Spain), where all those olive orchards are. It's a large place covering almost 34,000 square miles, which is about 17% of Spain. It is bordered on the west by Portugal and a part of the Atlantic Ocean. To the south and the east, it borders the Mediterranean Sea. Seville is the capital of the autonomous region.

A QUICK HISTORY OF ANDALUSIA

While not as old as Sicily (10,000BC), Andalusia dates to about 4,000BC. You will need to understand the region's history to take in the sites you will visit. It's not like Italy. Anyone can look at the Coliseum or the Roman Forum and say, "oh yes, it's the Romans or the Roman Empire." It's a different story when it comes to Andalusia. So here is an overview.

About the year 1,000BC, the Phoenicians established the port city of Cadiz. They called it Cadir. Cadiz still exists and is a major port city on the Atlantic. It is located just around the corner from Gibraltar and abutting Portugal. The Phoenicians were an ancient people from the city that is now known as Tunis.

About the year 500BC the Carthaginians and Greeks took hold of Andalusia and started developing towns. About 200BC, the Roman Empire moved in and created the Roman Province of Baetica. It wasn't until about 700AD when the Muslims (Moors) from Morocco moved in (it's only a few miles across the Straits of Gibraltar) and take some space from the Romans and Visigoths. The Moors called the land Al-Andalus.

About the year 900AD, the entire area south of the Castile-Leon northern area, i.e., Madrid-Toledo, was now Muslim Spain with its headquarter in Cordoba. About 1100AD Muslim Spain broke apart. The cities of

Seville and Cordoba, and others were constantly invaded by other Moorish tribes crossing the Mediterranean from North Africa. These invasions continued until about 1212AD.

About 1251AD, the Christians from Northern Spain (Castile-Leon) invaded the south and took back most of Andalusia, kicking out the Moors. And as we all know, in the year 1492AD, Queen Isabella and King Ferdinand declared Spain a Catholic country, and if you were not Catholic, you had to leave the country. If you cared not to go, you had to convert to Catholicism. While Jews were the predominant victims of the expulsion, thousands of Moors were also asked to leave or convert to Catholicism in subsequent years.

In summary, when you visit the major cities and sites of Andalusia, namely Cordoba, Granada, Seville, and Malaga, you will understand the heritage of this land. Many ancient sites are Muslim, some are Jewish, some are Christian, and some we just don't know anything about. I might note that before 1492AD, for a period of 500 years, Moors (Muslims), Jews, and Christians all lived in harmony on the Iberian Peninsula. So much for a short history of the area. Now let's get down to the land of Andalusia.

This Itinerary "C" is described as a week in Andalusia *originating in Madrid.* Suppose you are coming directly down to Seville from Barcelona (via the Madrid Bypass). In that case, you can follow this itinerary in reverse, i.e., from Seville, head north to Madrid, and visit Cordoba with a day trip to Granada. There are several direct trains to Cordoba from Barcelona. However, most of them require a connection in Madrid. If you come down from Barcelona, you will probably fly out of Madrid and do this itinerary in reverse, i.e., Seville, Cordoba, Granada (day trip), then Madrid. So now, let's rough out the week.

MADRID-ANDALUSIA ITINERARY C

ROUGH OUT
Day 1   Morning train Madrid to Cordoba
            Cordoba site seeing in the PM
Day 2   Day trip to Granada
            Plan on an optional extra day in Cordoba
Day 3   Morning train to Seville
Day 4   Second day site-seeing Seville
Day 5   Day trip to Morocco *
Day 6   Day trip to Ronda *
Day 7   Day trip to Gibraltar *
Day 8   Fly back to the USA/Canada from
            Seville or train back to Madrid

*Morocco, Ronda, and Gibraltar discussed in a separate chapter: Seville-Costa del Sol day trips

>>>TIP<<<

You will need to get train tickets for the AVE train from Madrid to Cordoba (mid-morning) before leaving North America. You can't afford to arrive in Madrid and find all trains in the morning sold out for your specific day's journey to Cordoba. See more later in this chapter. There are no pre-paid tickets required for any sites (the Mezquita) in Cordoba.
>>>>><<<<<

>>>TIP<<<

If you are taking the day trip to Granada, you must purchase your morning rail tickets from Cordoba to Granada (see below) before leaving North America. Like the Uffizi Gallery in Florence and other sites, you must purchase your tickets to the Alhambra (in Granada, not Cordoba) complex (Generalife) also online. It would help if you figured your entrance time about one hour after your train arrives in Granada. See more on this day trip below and one of my maps in the rear of this book.

Because trains between Cordoba and Granada are few, consider your day trip to Granada using the ALSA bus (coach). See below for details.
>>>>><<<<<

CORDOBA AND GRANADA

First, Cordoba is one of the three medieval (and sometimes many years earlier than the Medieval times) cities of Southern Spain, Andalusia. Along with Seville and Granada they are all UNESCO World Heritage Sites and are also in the book by Patricia Schultz *1,000 Places To See Before You Die.*

CORDOBA

Most of my friends and other people I have spoken to always confuse Cordoba with Granada. Both contain several Moorish (Islam) in addition to Christian sites. And, both are pretty old. Cordoba is the home of the Mezquita, which dates to about the year 700AD when the Moors took it over from the Visigoths. The Romans had already pulled out over 200 years ago. Here the Moors built a monumental mosque, the Mezquita. It subsequently became a Catholic cathedral in 1236AD after the Christian conquest from the North of Spain (Kingdom of Castile). It is the number one draw for visitors to see in Cordoba, in addition to the Jewish Quarter. There are other sites to see if time permits. These are the Roman Bridge and the Calahorra Tower.

GRANADA

Granada is the home of the Alhambra (note, it is not the Alah-Hambra but the Al-hambra). It is a complex of many buildings which date back to about 900AD. The complex contains a fortress (Alcazar), a Mosque, and many other unique buildings of beautiful art, fountains, and Moorish design. The complex is a walled city in itself containing 30 towers. The Alhambra sits on 26 acres. I have visited the Alhambra twice and can tell you; it is a must to see and don't miss the "Generalife." You can find all those details about the Alhambra at their website *Alhambra de Granada.org*

With respect to Cordoba and Granada, if you can spare another day, it would be worth spending it in Cordoba. Best to see the Mezquita and the Jewish Quarter on arrival in Cordoba, then take the day trip to Granada the next day. If you can spare another day, do see the other attractions in Cordoba.

THE CORDOBA-GRANADA CLIMATE & DRESS
If you are considering a trip to Spain from June 1 to September 30, you should realize that Cordoba and Granada are the hottest places in Spain during this time. It is not uncommon for temperatures to rise above 100 degrees Fahrenheit. However, it's not a big deal as all hotels, restaurants, and trains are air-conditioned. What you need to do is wear your sunscreen, wear hats, and dress lightly. I suggest men wear shorts and women wear "Capris," pants or pedal pushers. Many houses of worship i.e., churches, cathedrals, basilicas, mosques, and synagogues, do not allow women to wear skimpy shorts and no "short-shorts." Also, men usually cannot wear "tank tops."

Modesty must always be preserved. Best to check their websites. And do make sure you always have a bottle of water with you. So here we go-

Day 1 MORNING TRAIN TO CORDOBA

There are several trains a day to Cordoba. It's on the same line as Seville, which is the terminus of most of the high-speed AVE trains. Hopefully, you bought your reserved seat ticket already, and all you need do is make your way over to Atocha Station.

It is critical that you take a mid-morning train to take advantage of the afternoon to visit the Mezquita and the Jewish Quarter. Trains depart only from Madrid's Atocha station about every two hours. I always suggest you get a 9:30 AM or 11:30 AM train. These AVE trains are all reserved seat trains. So don't expect to arrive at the station at about 9:15 AM and purchase a ticket. Like Italy, in peak periods, all seats will be sold out, and if you are lucky, you will be on a train that evening or the next day. The reserved seat fare usually runs about 60 Euros and makes the run doing almost 200 mph in a little less than two hours. I might note that many times you will see Cordoba written with a "V," i.e., Cordova. Don't worry, it's the same place. I might note the same is true for Granada. You may find it also spelled as "Grenade." The Renfe website uses Grenade but converts it after you select it to Granada.

If this is your first AVE trip and you are not traveling Preferente (First Class), where you will get a meal, a light snack, and a glass of wine, you might want to arrive at least 45 minutes before your departure time to get some food to go at many of the take-out places in Atocha Station. Since you will already have had breakfast about an hour or two ago, you will only need some snacks and a bottle of water. Also, a feature of traveling Preferente Class is that you get to use the Preferente Class Lounge at Atocha, known as the Sala Lounge. You will find it past security. Just ask the security or Renfe reps where it is.

Keep your eye on the large orange lights on the departure board. When Cordoba or Cordova comes on, find your way to the Via (track number). Go thru security and make your way to the coach. Also, note that most AVE trains depart through the new modern side of the Atocha station. If you are in the Sala Lounge, train departures are shown on the TV monitors.

>>>TIP<<<
If this is your first AVE (or other high-speed reserved seat journey), remember, if you are running late, the best is to hop on any coach and "walk the train" to your assigned coach and seat. Don't be afraid to ask the train attendants for assistance. Most of them all speak a little English and will be happy to help you.
>>>>><<<<<

On arrival at Cordoba's modern train station, you will find it best to check into a hotel within a few blocks of the station. The station is relatively modern. Like New York's Penn Station and Grand Central, you arrive underground, and you will need to follow the crowds to the escalator, which will take you to the concourse and the main street level.

Since you will be returning to Cordoba station for your next leg of your Andalusia journey to Seville and your day trip to Granada, you will find it best to stay at a hotel within a 5-10 minute walk to the station. In this way, you will not have to take a taxi to and from your hotel to reach the station.

Here are my suggested hotels within a 10 minute, easy walk to the station. This area is relatively flat:
AC Hotel 4 star 3 blocks, it's a Marriott
Hotel Cordoba Center 4 star 4 blocks
TRYP Cordoba 3 Star, 5 blocks

Now if you just have carry-ons, consider these hotels, else take a taxi for four Euros. They are still only less than a 15-minute walk from the rail station. Great for that day trip to Granada:

15 MINUTE WALK HOTELS
Directions in short for all three hotels-
Leave the station and go down Av de los Mozarabes

Take the left between the parks (Hiroshima Nag)
Take the first right on Paseo de la Victoria. You will find all three of the hotels listed below within a few blocks of each other.

Hotel Selu, 3 Star, 10 minute walk (My choice)
NH Cordoba Califa, 3 Star, 13 minute walk
Eurostars Palace 5 Star, 15 minutes (at end of park)

>>>TIP<<<
After checking into your hotel or just dropping your bags at the hotel because your room is not ready, head directly over to the Mezquita-Cathedral. There are numerous cafes and stand-up tapas bars abutting the Mezquita-Cathedral area. Best you have a quick bite here before your entrance to the Mezquita.
>>>>><<<<<

After you enjoy that tapas, walk across the street and figure an hour to two hours to take in this beautiful building with all those hundreds of colorful arches. As of now, there is an 11 Euro entrance fee. You can enquire more about headsets and a docent escort when you arrive. Because of Covid-19 there is a limitation of the number of people allowed in the Mosque-Cathedral. So best is to visit their website at mezquita-catedraldecordoba.es/en/. Make sure you are accessing the official site.

Also, realize that the Mezquita is now a Roman Catholic Cathedral (since 1236AD) and operates daily and Sunday Masses. There are lots to see here and do take plenty of photos. Do invest in the audio tour or use the services of one of the docents. It will be well worth the money. After you visit the Mezquita, find your way over (just a few blocks) to the Old Jewish Quarter and walk the small cobblestone streets.

If you are of the Jewish Persuasion, I always suggest visiting one of the oldest Jewish Synagogues in Spain. While you are there, do not fail to take pictures at the statue of Moses Maimonides (the "Rambam") located directly in front of the Synagogue. Maimonides was a rabbi, physician, astronomer, and philosopher. He was quite a guy for his time (about 60 years prior to 1200AD." There are hundreds of writings on his life and his contributions to Jewry and humanity.

Turning back to Cordoba, this is one place "where you can't get there from here." Worse, it's like a jigsaw puzzle with a maze of one-way streets and is extremely difficult to navigate around. Best walk it if you can.

I don't know if there will be time to see Cordoba's other sites, which is why I recommend, if possible, a second day, preferably after your day trip to Granada. The other sites most often visited are the Roman Bridge with its Calahora tower, the Alcazar de los Reyes Christianos, and the Patio de los Naranjos.

For the best shopping and dinner, I recommend the Historic District. It's easy to find. If you come out of the Eurostars Maimonides Hotel, take a left, go about 20 yards right past the garage to the hotel, then take a right and walk 100 meters (about a football field), the Mezquita will be on your right, you will find the district opposite the long block of the Mezquita. At night the streets of this district are all lit up and make great photos—lots of restaurants and shops. Do watch out for the glazed tile walkways in the rain, as they can be somewhat slippery.

On your next day, you are going to take a day trip to Granada. I say a day trip because Granada is only 90 minutes away (by rail) and "off the beaten track." You will only need 4-6 hours here as other than the Alhambra and Generalife, there is not much outside of the Alhambra complex to see, other than hotels and restaurants. Suppose you do want to make Granada an overnight trip. My only recommendation is the Parador of Granada in the Alhambra complex and the Hotel America, which is also in the complex. Once again spend the money, it's an experience!

Day 2 DAY TRIP TO GRANADA

You can understand the Moorish (Islam) impact on the Iberian Peninsula when you visit the Alhambra. The architecture and the mosaic artwork are incredible. There are many buildings here in addition to the magnificent gardens of the Generalife. There is an awful lot of walking since the complex is built on a hill. While escalators help, be prepared to be "pooped" by the end of the day and enjoy that train ride back.

To plan the day properly, you need to do two things before you leave the USA or Canada:
Buy your rail tickets or your ALSA bus tickets:
I won't discuss too much on a rail day trip because the timing each way is horrible. It's probably because of Covid, and hopefully, the schedule will get better when the pandemic is over. The frequency of trains here in Andalusia is nothing like the Madrid and Barcelona areas, and certainly not like Italy!

So your best alternative is the ALSA bus. It's air-conditioned, has a toilette, WIFI, and movies to watch. Takes about 2.5 hours. It's actually one of those touring coaches. So just leave your bags in your room, grab your day bag and head out to the bus terminal. YOU MUST MAKE A RESERVATION ONLINE BEFORE YOU LEAVE THE USA/CANADA. These guys at ALSA know what they are doing! Here is the daily schedule:

Lv Cordoba- 8:30am arrives 11:00am 2.5 hrs 8Euros
Lv Granada- 18:00(6pm) arrives 20:30 (8:30PM) 8Euros

The schedule is meant for tourists. Make sure you bring some snacks. Also, the coach outbound to Granada makes several stops in Cordoba. Ask your hotel concierge or front desk clerk where is the best place to pickup the bus. All seats are reserved. To be on the safe side best to board the bus at the origination station.

Another idea is to do a combination of the train to Granada and take the ALSA bus back. There is an early train at about 10 AM to Granada. The train will get you into Granada at about 11:45 AM and only cost you about $40. Figure about a 12:30 PM admission to the Alhambra-Generalife. On the return, the ALSA bus departs about 6 PM from the bus station in Granada. You must make a reservation in the USA/Canada about 30-45 days before; else, you will need to hunt down a toothbrush, underwear, and a hotel for your unexpected overnight stay in Granada.

Now here is another rail alternative, if you don't want to take the 2.5 hour coach ride or rail out and coach back. Instead of a day trip, it's a departure from Cordoba with an overnight stop in Granada and then on to Seville. You should allow for that second day in Cordoba before you head out for Granada and Seville.

RAIL TO GRANADA THEN ON TO SEVILLE

On your second day in Cordoba, return to your hotel about noon, grab your bags, and head over to the Cordoba rail station. There is usually a train (of course for the tourists) at about 1:30 PM (13:30 exactly), which goes over to Granada. The run is less than 90 minutes on the AVE and will cost you 20-30 Euros. By the time you grab a café and look at some scenery or take a snooze, the train will be in Granada. On arrival at the rail station, take a taxi to your hotel. It should not be more than ten Euros.

If you can book the early train, about 10 AM from Cordoba, it would be far better. Taking the earlier train will allow you to see the Alhambra on arrival, spend the evening in Granada and then take the train the next day in the morning or mid-afternoon. If you are taking the **ALSA** coach from Cordoba to Granada, it is large and will carry your bags in the bus's belly.

>>>TIP<<<
Get your rail or bus tickets first and plan your journey. Should it be a day trip, or should you go to Seville directly from Granada? The Alhambra tickets are "timed"; however, don't be concerned if you arrive too late or too early. They will still allow you entry.
>>>>><<<<<

I favor (only because I know the area) the Parador of Granada. It's a four-star hotel and actually on the grounds of the Alhambra. Another hotel which borders on a country inn, also on the grounds of the Alhambra is, the Hotel America. It is a one-star hotel, but my feeling is that it should not be rated because it is not a hotel, but a country inn. Do check it out.

If you stay at the Parador or the Hotel America in the Alhambra itself, you probably will go out for dinner. Some of the Paradors do offer dinner. You can email then before arrival as to their dinner offerings, if any.

As an alternative, you will find dozens of hotels off the Carrera del Darro and the Calle San Juan de los Reyes.

If you are doing the Granada to Seville by train instead of a day trip out of Cordoba, you will need to visit the Alhambra right after breakfast, about 10 AM. Check your bags with the bellman since you will have to retrieve them at about 2 PM for your train to Seville at about 14:52 (2:52 PM). Once again, this train late in the day is operated for the tourists, now onto Seville.

SEVILLE HIGHLIGHTS
Seville is one of my favorite cities in all of Western Europe. I have been there four times and can't say enough about it. I just love their boulevards lined with orange trees and the old Santa Cruz district. La

Albahaca is one of my favorite restaurants in Seville, which serves up outstanding Andalusian Spanish cuisine; it lies right next to the best Flamenco club in all of Spain (Los Gallos). If you enjoyed the Casa Botin in Madrid, you would love La Albahaca. Prices have changed over the years, as I believe they may have a prix fixed menu now. Also, suggest you check reviews.

>>>TIP<<<

It is best to see the Flamenco show next door to La Albahaca first at 8 PM. Have your drinks there and then in about 90 minutes, walk next door to La Albahaca and have dinner. You will need a reservation at Los Gallos and one at La Albahaca. You need to queue up at Los Gallos at 7:30 PM for the evening's first show. You can buy your tickets online: http://www.tablaolosgallos.com/en/the-tablao/. Call ahead to confirm show availability on date and times. As an alternative to dinner, enjoy the flamenco show first and then a light dinner of tapas and Sangria in one of the local eateries in the Santa Cruz Barrio. This area, as well as most of Seville, is relatively safe. Consider walking back to your hotel near the Bario Santa Cruz.
>>>>><<<<<

You will need two full days in Seville. Anything less you will be missing a lot. If you are coming down from Cordoba, Granada, or Madrid you should plan to arrive before 2 PM. You can consider this your first day. Here is what you need to take in on your two day visit:

WHAT TO SEE IN SEVILLE

When I first saw the Alcazar of Seville (sometimes known as the Real Alcazar), it reminded me of pictures of the Hanging Gardens of Babylon. This Alcazar is nothing like the Alcazars of Toledo and Segovia, which are fortresses. This Alcazar was a palace and now has been restored to its glory. Of course, it is a **UNESCO World Heritage Site**. The original palace dates to about 700AD when the Moors invaded Iberia and conquered Seville. Over the years, the Spanish Catholic Kings, who drove out the Moors, took over the Palace about the 12th Century and expanded it to what it is now. The Catholic Kings from Castile-Leon in the north kept the original palace buildings and gardens, which were the original Moorish (Islamic) Mudejar style. This style is the same (arches and mosaics) and the artwork you have already seen in Cordoba and Granada.

>>>TIP<<<

To avoid being shut out of visiting the Alcazar of Seville, you should purchase your tickets 6-8 weeks before your visit or as soon as they become available. The fee is about 10 Euros. Do include the audio headsets in your reservation or rent them on site. Their website is www.alcazarsevilla.org.
>>>>><<<<<

The number two site I recommend seeing is the Cathedral de Seville. Like many of the Catholic cathedrals in Italy and Spain, it is an architectural masterpiece. Of most importance is the tomb of Columbus. Supposedly, the reason the tomb is raised is that Columbus did not want to be buried on Spanish soil. Contrary to most writings, Columbus never sailed to the "New World" from Seville. He sailed from the nearby cities, which still exist today, Cadiz and Huelva.

A few feet from the Cathedral lies the famous Giralda tower (Torre Giralda). If you have the energy, you can climb it. I do caution seniors with mobility or heart conditions. You can take great photos of the City from the top. There is a small fee to climb the Tower, and you do not have to make reservations. The nice thing about the Tower is that it has 35 ramps and only 17 steps at the top. Suggest you do not climb the Tower right after lunch; do it before lunch and take your time!

The Plaza de Espana is worth a visit. This place is not, repeat, not ancient. It was built in 1928 for the 1929 Ibero-American Exposition; the complex is located in the Parque de Maria Luisa. It is just too difficult to explain all the details about this beautiful building and the rest of the complex. However, I might note that it appears in all those photos of Seville, right up there with the Alcazar, Giralda Tower, Cathedral of Seville, and the Barrio Santa Cruz.

The fifth major attraction is the Barrio Santa Cruz. The Barrio used to be the old Jewish Quarter of Seville. If you are not having dinner at La Albahaca, the best is to visit the Barrio after your nap; do your shopping here and then have dinner. The Barrio is what makes Europe.. Europe. Outdoor cafes, cobblestone streets, and streets (alleys) you can't get a car through. Where in America can you find this? Make sure you don't get lost, and for heaven's sake, do not pick the oranges. This place is loaded with shops, restaurants and is the original Seville. The Barrio is where you want to take those great photos, especially at night. Abutting the Barrio, you will also find my favorite hotel, Hotel Fernando III. Fernando is a four-star hotel, even with a rooftop pool. So much for an overview of Seville.

GRANADA TO SEVILLE BY TRAIN
It will cost you about $60-90 depending on the train and the time. They are all fast AVE trains and will make the journey in about 2.5 hours. As always, make sure you have enough snacks and water for the trip. There is very limited shopping at the station in Granada and only one café to grab a sandwich.

>>>TIP<<<
I recommend arriving early at the station and going across the street to the "Mercodona" supermarket. Here you will find those snacks and water. Do watch your time as you don't want to miss that train to Seville.

Best also to have your partner watch your bags at the train station while one of you runs across the street.
>>>>><<<<<

From here, jump down to the section "***ON ARRIVAL IN SEVILLE***"

CORDOBA TO SEVILLE BY TRAIN

If you are coming down from Cordoba to Seville, because the run is only 45 minutes on the AVE train, you will find it best to take the morning train at about 10:30 AM or the 1:30 PM train. Bear in mind that all of these trains come down from Madrid. You will only be able to reserve seats for passengers disembarking in Cordoba and usually one intermediate station. Therefore, it is critical to make your train reservations as soon as those dates of travel open up at Renfe. The fare runs $14-40 depending on the train.

>>>TIP<<<

Seville is one place you do not want to "short" your time. As stated earlier, I recommend two full days of site-seeing. However, I have always felt that Seville is one of those romantic, if not the most romantic city in Spain. Best to get the AVE train at the lower price of $14 (check renfe.com schedules) and put that extra money (instead of the $40 fare) toward a few more days in Seville. There are also several day trips from Seville that I have covered under a separate chapter.
>>>>><<<<<

From here, jump down to the section "*** ON ARRIVAL IN SEVILLE ***."

MADRID TO SEVILLE BY TRAIN
Renfe operates trains from Atocha as well as Chamartin stations. They are all AVE or AVANT, fast trains which make the journey to Seville (with just a few quick stops) in about 2 hours and 40 minutes. If you want to take that 7 AM train, it will cost about $25; later trains will cost about $80-$100. Outside of Barcelona-Madrid, it is one of Renfe's most popular routes. There are about ten trains a day. All trains, are reserved seats.

>>>TIP<<<
You will find a limited amount of trains into Seville's San Bernardo (Bernard) station compared to Santa Justa. Also, you may have to change trains. So, the best is to go directly to Santa Justa, the main station.
>>>>><<<<<

>>>TIP<<<
If this is your first AVE experience, make sure you arrive early (allow 45 minutes) before departure. One hour would even be better. This Seville departure you do not want to miss. Before leaving your hotel, make sure you have sandwiches or snacks and that bottle of water. You will also find at Atocha and Chamartin stations many places for "take-a-way" bocadillo's (sandwiches) and other delights.

Now, keep your eye on the departure board with all those orange lights for your train destination and time. If you are departing from Atocha you need to go over to the new side (not the side with all the commuter trains). The train information people will help you or follow the crowd when they post your train info on the board.

*** ON ARRIVAL IN SEVILLE ***
All trains arrive at the new modern train station in Seville, known as Santa Justa. When you arrive, you will need to take a taxi to your hotel, preferably in or around the Barrio Santa Cruz. It will cost you about 7-9 Euros.

There are several other train stations in Seville. Like Cordoba, trains arrive at Santa Justa underground. You will have to take an escalator to the main level, exit, and then follow the signs to the taxi queue. If you want to purchase any items for souvenirs and feel you won't have enough time at the airport, this station is the place. The concourse level (just above the tracks) is loaded with shops and eateries.

>>>TIP<<<
Seville has lots of modern high-rise hotels. These hotels are used for conferences, conventions, and what the Europeans call "Congresses." It is best not to stay at these hotels. They are just too large and too commercial. Your best bet is to stay in and around the quaint old Santa Cruz district, also known as Barrio

Santa Cruz. See below for my recommendations. For many of you, Seville will be your last stop before flying home, unless you are going on to the Costa del Sol area for an actual "vacation." You know the type where you plunk yourself at a lovely beach resort hotel. So, for now, you need not locate yourself at a hotel around the Santa Justa rail station.
>>>>><<<<<

Here are some hotels in or around the Barrio:
Just a note, the new Tram system does not actually go into the Barrio district, although it does come close to the Cathedral. Besides, a new subway was added a few years ago called the "Seville Metro." It is best to check with your hotel concierge if you can use it to get around the city since it is minimal. You will find most of the attractions in or around the Barrio.

Hotel Fernando III 4 Star – Rooftop pool
   This is my favorite and I do recommend it.
Catalonia Giralda 4 Star- Indoor pool
Hotel Rey Alfonso X 4 Star
Hotel Alacantara 2 Star
Byron Suites 4 Star
El Rey Moro Hotel 3 Star
Hotel Murillo 2 Star
Hotel Goya 2 Star
Hotel Casa 1800 Sevilla 4 Star
Casa del Poeta 4 Star

There are many more....

Suppose you arrive early enough and have your reservations for the Alcazar the following day. In that case, my suggestion is to walk over to the Cathedral and pay your respects to Columbus along with seeing this beautiful Cathedral. If you have the energy after sitting on the train, consider climbing the Giralda Tower. It's right next to the Cathedral.

Enjoy the Barrio Have a café, some tapas, and do some shopping before returning to your hotel for a snooze before dinner at about 8 PM.

When you are finished with visiting the highlights of Seville, consider some of the day trips from Seville. You will find them in a separate chapter.

If you are flying home from Seville, you will need to make your way to the airport. Sorry to say, there is no train or subway to the Seville (SVQ) airport. Best to give it another ten years, and they will probably have one. Here are my suggestions to get you and your bags to the airport:

A taxi will cost you about 28 Euros. The fare is fixed. When you have your hotel concierge call the taxi company, ask them for the fixed rate to the airport. Also, advise them when booking if you will be paying with a credit card or cash.

Other than a taxi, several buses run back and forth from the Seville airport. However, bear in mind that you probably will have to go over to a bus departure point:

TUSSAM BUS- Also known as the EA bus
The Tussam Bus is a sweet deal. The Tussam operates every 15 minutes at the cost of only 4 Euros per person. You pay onboard. It makes several stops in the City before heading directly to the airport. Best to check pickup points and departure times with your hotel concierge. The "EA" bus takes about 35 minutes.

It would be best if you allowed plenty of time before your flight to reach the airport, as buses may be crowded in peak periods of the day or week.

If you wish to do some of the day trips out of Seville or go on to Malaga and the Costa del Sol consult those chapters. If not, enjoy your fly out from Seville Airport back to the USA or Canada.

CHAPTER 10

MALAGA-MARBELLA AND THE COSTA DEL SOL (CDS)

ITINERARY "D"

INTRODUCTION

I made my first trip to the Costa del Sol area in 1976. There was a firm based in Boston called "International Weekends." They advertised a charter flight, one week (basis of two people), in a hotel with a kitchen and buffet breakfast each morning. Get this, and the cost was only $395 a person—what a deal. In six weeks, I was sitting on the beach in "Benalmadena" on the CDS. I have since gone back to the area about seven times and can't believe how this place has grown. I have stayed at hotels, done those time-shares, and most recently rented an apartment in Calahonda. I have seen ads in the British newspapers stating that you can live cheaper for one week (including meals) on the Costa del Sol than you can in London. It's still true today.

What makes CDS so popular today is the number of flights from all over, which go in and out of Malaga (airport code is AGP), the new recently modernized and expanded airport which serves the area. In addition, the new high-speed AVE trains all run from various parts of Spain to Malaga Zambrano station. The Cercanias (commuter) C1 (and C2) rounds out the public transportation in the area. The beach communities from Malaga to Fuengirola are served by the C1 line, which I might add also stops at the airport. With about 18 stops on the C1 line, you do not need to rent a car. The Spanish Government has created a resort area that is far superior to our Southeast Florida (West Palm Beach to Miami) corridor. When you get off the C1 line, all you need do is walk a few blocks to your hotel. They couldn't have made it more convenient.

The C1 line will be extended to Marbella and hopefully Estepona in the West and Nerja in the east in the next few years. If you want to go to Marbella, you must take a bus from the end of the C1 line in Fuengirola. The extension to Marbella will start shortly.

Toward the east side of Malaga, there is only bus service to the smaller beach communities.

If you are considering a month away during the cold winter weather in the US or Canada, consider CDS, where you can rent an apartment for under $1500 a month within walking distance to the C1 line, banks, pharmacies, and grocery stores, and yes with a pool.

For decades, the CDS area has been a haven for "Brits" and others from the cold north of Europe. My second time to the area, I stayed again in Benalmadena and was amazed that you could get an English Breakfast consisting of toast, two eggs, and "bangers" for about two pounds (about $5). What a deal. The same goes for dinner, where the tourist menu of the day (Table d' Hote) goes for about $8, including a Pynt (sic) of beer.

Except for Mijas and a few sites in Malaga, this is one place where you can relax by the side of the pool or take a dip in the Med after that exhausting week or two touring Spain. Trust me you will need it.

I can recommend four real points of interest. They are the hill-top town of Mijas which is excellent for dinner and shopping in the early evening; a trip to the Picasso Museum in Malaga; the caves at Nerjas; and the day to explore the history of the walled city of Malaga and also take a horse and carriage ride for two.

If you are shopping, Malaga is the place. Lots and lots of shopping here where you will find everything from food to clothing. If you have never been to a Primark store, this is the place. There are two of them. So, no need to go to London or Dublin. Best that you buy another suitcase or a duffel bag to take all that Primark clothing home. You will need it.

I might add there are several flea (or outdoor food markets), sometimes just called street markets, in the area on different days. Best to check out also before you take off for the Picasso Museum for the day. My favorites are the ones in Marbella and Torremolinos. There are also street markets in Estepona, Nerjas and Benalmadena. It is best to check the internet in your planning stage for days of operation of the street fairs.

By far, the best one in the area is Marbella. It is located in the Puerto Banus area on the Calle Pilar Calvu. This boulevard abuts the Marbella Bullring and runs for about ten city blocks. Lots of clothing here and really nice items, and I don't mean T-shirts! I have never been to **CDS** without attending the Saturday street market in Marbella (Puerto Banus).

If you are not staying in Marbella, you will have to take a local bus or a taxi over to the bullring. There are buses to Marbella from the terminus of the C1 line in Fuengirola. The local buses traveling the main road, the "340," all stop at the interchange at the base of the Calle Pilar Calvu. Just follow the crowd off the bus.

I prefer and always have stayed in later years in the upscale Marbella area. However, for now, as I stated before, you will need to take the bus from the C1 Cercanias station in Fuengirola. In summary, it is best to stay within a 5-10 walk of the closest C1 station. The bus takes only 15 minutes, else pile four in a taxi.

If you are attending the street market in Torremolinos, which I believe is the next best to Marbella, it is held on Thursdays and is also located next to a bullring (in Torremolinos). If you stay in Torremolinos, no problem, else you will have to take the train to the end of the C1 line in Torremolinos and then walk about 20 minutes over to the bullring or hop a taxi for five Euros.

ROUGH OUT FOR THE WEEK IN CDS
Day 1- Friday, Arrive in the Costa del Sol
Day 2- Saturday- the street market at Marbella near the bullring
Day 3- Sunday – Tangier Morocco/easy day on the beach or shopping in Malaga
Day 4- Monday- Day trip Ronda (avoid Sundays)
Day 5- Tuesday- The Picasso Museum & Malaga Horse carriage 90 minute tour
Day 6- Wednesday- Day trip to Gibraltar
Day 7- Thursday- the street market at Torremolinos Also near the bullring.
Day 8- Friday the caves at Nerjas.
Day 9- Fly home from Malaga Airport (AGP)

Take a look first at the Seville and CDS day trips chapter before you plan on going to the CDS area. You might want to consider a "swing thru" or an overnighter, perhaps in **Ronda**, before going on to Marbella and the other CDS communities. Consult some of my maps in the back of this book.

>>>TIP<<<
It would be best if you planned your day visits in the cool morning and "lounged" on the beach or next to the pool in the warm afternoon.
>>>>><<<<<

Before considering another Spain week in the CDS area, you might want to check out air arrangements, especially if you are using frequent flyer tickets since many frequent flyer plans do not include "secondary cities," i.e., American Airlines does not fly to Malaga. So you may have to fly in and out of Madrid on a frequent flyer plan and purchase a local one-way ticket from Malaga to Madrid, which is relatively inexpensive. If you are in the CDS area, the best is to take the AVE train to Madrid. It will be less time and less stress.

>>>TIP<<<
If you must return to Madrid for your long-haul flight back to North America, don't chance a rail journey early in the morning to Atocha with a rail connection to Barajas Airport. It is best to position yourself at the

Madrid Barajas airport the night before. On arrival at Atocha, take the train to the airport (see the chapter on Madrid-Barcelona), then take the free shuttle bus to one of the airport hotels. I recommend the IBIS at the airport. It's actually in the village of Barajas abutting the airport. It is inexpensive, and they have a free shuttle service to and from the airport.
>>>>><<<<<

With respect to your days in the CDS area, if you need to eliminate days, skip the Morocco trip and the Caves at Nerja. Do visit Ronda, the street markets in Marbella (Puerto Banus) or Torremolinos.

You can shop and have dinner in the quaint little town of Mijas (actually Mijas Pueblo) any day of the week. Remember, dinner is usually at 8 PM. Also, do not forget the donkey ride. You will also have to arrive by taxi or better, there is also a bus from the Fuengirola bus station to Mijas Pueblo. See your concierge or hotel desk clerk for the current schedule.

>>>TIP<<<

CDS is a place where you definitely want to layout the week. First, see if you can attend the street market in Marbella, definitely a must on Saturday. Do that day trip to Ronda and Gibraltar, and remember many of the shops are closed on Sunday. So, you need to visit Ronda and Gibraltar midweek. The Picasso museum

is open every day of the week, best for a rainy day, although very rare. In summary, if you are coming to the CDS either from Seville or Madrid, better to plan the week before you come down.
>>>>><<<<<

>>>TIP<<<
Before committing to a room at a hotel, time-share, an Airbnb, condo rental, or whatever, it is best to ask what the closest C1 station is and how far is the walk. You can also check it out on Google Maps. If you are self-catering in a rental, check out the closest grocery, i.e., Supermercado, Mercadona, etc.
>>>>><<<<<

HOW TO GET TO THE COSTA DEL SOL AREA

If this is your second or third week in Spain and the end of your visit, you should consider flying out of Malaga (AGP). Flying from Malaga eliminates the problem of getting back to Madrid or Barcelona. You can connect in most of the major cities in Europe, i.e., Malaga to Munich, then on to Newark airport in New Jersey.

If you are coming from SEVILLE:
4-5 Trains a day all AVE except a connection of
an AVE and an AVANT usually in the evening
The run time is 2 hours
It costs about $50. The evening connection is about $10 less and takes 2.5 hours

If you are coming from **MADRID**:
4-5 Trains a day all AVE from ATOCHA
The run time is 2 hours, 50 minutes
It costs, depending on the train, $55-70.
Note, there are no trains from Chamartin.

If you are coming from **BARCELONA**:
6 Trains a day, all AVE, all with connections, except the late afternoon train, which is a direct train. You will probably have to change in Madrid or Zaragoza with the connections. Suggest you pay the extra $15-20 and take the direct train. Prices are $85-100, and this is definitely the long haul. Run time is about 6 hours with the direct and about 6.5-7 hours on the connections.

If you are coming from **GRANADA**:
This is probably one of those stop-overs since you are probably not originating your Spain visit in Granada. There is a mid-day train at about 1:30PM (1320). It's a short 90 minute run to Malaga with lovely scenery and only costs $20. The fast **ADVANT** train is used.

If you are coming from **RONDA**:
Ronda is probably also one of those stop-overs since you are probably not originating your Spain visit in Ronda. Sorry, Ronda does not have an airport. Since COVID has had a significant impact on the tourist trade in Spain, there is only one train right now from Ronda to Malaga. The morning train leaves about 8

AM and arrives about two hours later in Malaga. However, you will probably have to change trains in "Antequera." There is a combination of the MD (Medium Distance) and the Avant trains. The price is about $18. Best to check the Renfe website as I am sure they will be adding more trains.

IF YOU ARE FLYING INTO MALAGA AIRPORT

This is an easy one since the C1 Cercanias line out of Malaga stops at the Malaga Airport. To find the C1 line, make your way to Terminal 3 and take the escalators or elevator downstairs. Purchase your ticket from the machines and follow the signs to trains to "Fuengirola" and not Malaga, unless you are staying in Malaga. Also, remember that Malaga has two stations, the Renfe rail station known as Zambrano and the last stop known as Centro.

IF YOU ARE ARRIVING BY TRAIN

You will arrive at the Zambrano Estacion. Follow the signs to the C1 Cercanias line. Its symbol is a red circle with a backward "C" in it. You can't miss it. Purchase your tickets from the machine and make sure you get the train going in the correct direction, probably "FUENGIROLA", unless it has already been extended to Marbella. Many beach communities have several stops. Make sure your hotel tells you which is the closest stop and if you require a taxi or a short walk.

>>>TIP<<<

You can purchase C1 tickets for the zone you want to travel to with your credit card. Consult the Zone chart at the station. Also, most stations have a "Reviewer" who will be able to help you out. Also, many Renfe rail tickets allow you a little over an hour to use your intercity ticket on any Cercanias route. Check with the ticket agent if you can wave your ticket at the turnstyle.
>>>>><<<<<

>>>TIP<<<

Make sure you hold that C1 ticket. You probably will need it to exit the C1 line (same as Paris). If you are over the zone charge, you will need to pay a surcharge at the machine before you exit.
>>>>><<<<<

DEPARTING THE CDS AREA:

After your stay in CDS, you will be flying back home or taking the train somewhere else in Spain. Here is what you need to do. Just reverse your direction:

Take the C1 line in the direction of Malaga. If you are flying, exit the train at Malaga airport and follow directions to your check-in counter. Consult the TV monitors on exiting the C1 line.

If you are continuing to other points in Spain or Madrid, exit the C1 train at Malaga Zambrano (the

Renfe rail station) and follow the signs to the check-in desk or ask any **Renfe** attendant for assistance.

Enjoy your trip home or your further travels in Spain.

CHAPTER 11

SEVILLE & COSTA DEL SOL DAY TRIPS

RONDA, GIBRALTAR AND TANGIER MOROCCO

RONDA (a/k/a ROUND)

I have always enjoyed day trips to Ronda (Round). I don't know what it is about this place. However, I do know it dates to about 600BC. There are lots of things to see and do: First, the shopping is incredible. I mean real bargains on shoes and women's leather boots, made in Spain and not in China. Shopping here is not a street fair. There are other stores which sell everything from kids' toys to clothing. And yes, you can buy those magnets for the refrigerator, the coffee mugs, and let's not forget all those Spanish-made leather belts.

It's pretty easy to find the major tourist shopping here. By the way, the locals shop here also. You will find all those streets running into the main boulevard, Calle

Arminan, which crosses the monster gorge. The streets are strictly for pedestrians are Calle Rosario (which becomes Calle Ermita), Calle Nueva, and Carrera Espinel. In addition to the shops, there are loads of cafes and eateries, and yes, there are several gelato shops. Don't worry, if you are coming from the central bus station you will be walking through the shopping district on one of the streets named above. From the bus terminal in Ronda, it is only a 10-minute walk to the Parador (hotel). Ronda is all flat, so walking should not be a problem if you are somewhat challenged. If you are arriving from Malaga on the direct train, you will find the rail station just 2 blocks from the bus terminal.

The second attraction in Ronda is what I call the Monster Gorge. You can't miss it. If you can find the Parador hotel (find the Parador, i.e., "Dond-day esta Parador?) you will find the gorge. It abuts the Parador on the Calle Arminan just past the Plaza Espana. Walk across the Puente Nuevo bridge. It's the new bridge, but it always looks old to me! Make sure you don't drop your camera or smartphone. Trust me on this one; you won't be able to retrieve it. From the top of the bridge, it's about one football field down. Yes, about 300 feet.

Did you know that Ronda is the birthplace of bullfighting? The bullring dates to 1785. It is centrally located about two blocks from the Parador. In addition to the bullring, there is also a bullfighting museum. It's sort of an odd museum since you probably have not seen one in the world. If you have some spare time, you can easily spend an hour here. The museum charges a fee of only two Euros. A deal!

Now here is how you get to Ronda from either Seville or the CDS area.

>>>TIP<<<
Try to avoid visiting Ronda on a Sunday as many of the shops may be closed.
>>>>><<<<<

SEVILLE TO RONDA (ROUND)

The bus (coach) trip from Seville to Ronda is 2.5 hours and only 90 minutes on the return. I don't know why. After the COVID pandemic is over, there hopefully will be bus in the morning, taking only 90 minutes.

If you miss the last bus out of Ronda in the early evening (around 6 PM), be prepared to spend the night here, not a bad idea. It is best to pack your toothbrush, a change of underwear, and ladies, your cosmetic bag in your day bag before leaving Seville in the morning. It would be best if you considered staying at the Parador or the Hotel Acinipo across from the bullring. Both are four-star hotels. There are many three-star hotels in the area, all within walking distance from the Parador located on the Plaza Espana.

DAMAS bus lines, which can be booked through Busbud.com, allow you to secure your round trip bus tickets directly. This is strongly advisable. Don't be shut out during peak periods. Because of tourists taking day trips to Ronda there 10 AM bus is usually booked early. It arrives in Ronda at about 12:15 PM. On the return, the last bus is at 6:30 PM and arrives back in Seville at 7:15 PM, leaving enough time for a snooze before dinner. Buses depart and arrive at the central Seville bus station on Prado de San Sebastian. You should verify this with your hotel clerk or concierge. The price is $16 each way. Verify all with the concierge on your arrival in Seville and not the night before your planned visit. Many times, the bus may be sold out if you have not purchased your tickets online.

While I always favor rail, I can emphatically state that the rail journey from Seville to Ronda will take you 3-4 hours and cost you about $40 each way. There are several connections and stops, and the schedule is "spotty." So best to stick with the bus. As an alternate, you can also try www.blablacar.com. Best if you get another couple to join you.

I find it better to do "swing through" Ronda on the way to the CDS. You are already halfway there. See my tip below.

COSTA DEL SOL (CDS) TO RONDA

If you stay in the CDS area, you will find it a little easier to get to Ronda than from Seville. First, you should note that the C1 Cercanias (commuter) line out of Malaga, which has many stops along the CDS beach resort communities, will be expanded from its present terminus in Fuengirola to Marbella in the next 2-3 years. This extension to Marbella will save about 30 minutes off of the current bus trip ride when taking the bus from Marbella instead of Fuengirola. Stay tuned.

Now, getting to Ronda from the CDS depends just where you are on the CDS. Suppose you stay in the Marbella area (because the C1 rail line has not been extended yet). In that case, there are about four daily buses to Ronda from the central bus station located on Avenida Trapiche in Marbella by Avanza (informacion@avanzabus.com). I believe it also stops in Puerto Banus an upscale community on the west side of Marbella where the Saturday street market is before heading to San Pedro Alcantara and on into the mountains. The two buses are called the L525 (which goes on to Seville) and the L304. The fare is a reasonable $15 each way. You will need to take a taxi over to the new bus station as it is not in the Golden Mile area of Marbella. It's on the other side of A7/340.

It would be best to get the first bus out in the morning at about 9:30 AM and the last bus out of Ronda back to

Marbella in the late afternoon or early evening. Depending on the schedule, the bus makes the run in about one hour, fifteen minutes, or two hours. If you are planning on a day visit to Ronda, I would strongly suggest that you get your bus tickets online before you leave North America, else you risk being shut out.

>>>TIP<<<
When you board the bus, try to get a seat on the driver's side. There are breathtaking views of the mountains. The door side hugs the mountains, so you really won't be able to see too much. On the return ride, favor the door side for the view over the mountains and sunset.
>>>>><<<<<

>>>TIP<<<
If you are using the services of BlaBlaCar, about 10 miles before you get to Ronda, there are a few cafes selling products of the area and snacks. The restrooms are clean. Just ask your BlaBlaCar driver to make a rest stop and do buy him a café. My favorite is the one on the right-hand side of the road known as "Venta La Higuera." Your driver should know where it is.
>>>>><<<<<

If you wish to make the journey by rail, you must work your way via the C1 Cercanias line over to the central train station in Malaga known as Zambrano (second to last stop). At Malaga Zambrano, you must take a high-speed intercity train to usually Antequera and change for the train to Ronda. There is also a direct train. Best to check the Renfe website. It's a total rail time of about 3-4 hours and about $40 each way. So, best to take the bus. Also, consider once again www.blablacar.com and see if you can have another couple join you since the price will be less per person.

If you are staying at one of the beach communities, i.e., Malaga, Torremolinos, Benalmadena, or Fuengirola (and the smaller communities between them), you can go either way (toward Malaga or toward Fuengirola) on the C1 line to get a bus. However, the best is to go to Fuengirola via the C1 line, then walk over to the bus terminal and take the Avanza bus to Ronda.

So, in summary, you can get a bus from Marbella (directly) to Ronda and from any of the beach communities by going first to Fuengirola with the C1 Commuter line. As discussed, Fuengirola is now the last stop on the C1 Commuter (Cercanias) line. The C1 is accessible pretty much from any point west of Malaga. Trains run every 20 minutes in both directions and cost about 2-4 Euros per ride depending on the distance traveled. The automatic machines at the C1 stations will take your credit card.

Once at the end of the C1 line in Fuengirola, you need to walk only one block down Calle Alfonso XIII toward the Med to the Estación de Autobuses to get your bus to Ronda. Allow 30 minutes before bus departure.

>>>TIP<<<

Just a word about the C1 line: It's almost like an elevated subway line stopping at all the beach communities of the CDS. Make sure you get the train going in the correct direction. The first car is marked Malaga (note there are two stations in downtown Malaga), and in the opposite direction, the train is marked Fuengirola. If you visit Malaga, make sure you get the C1 line back to your beach community since there is also a C2 line that goes inland.
>>>>><<<<<

>>>TIP<<<

If you are making the day trip to Ronda from CDS, best to check out how and where you get the C1 line to Fuengirola. From Fuengirola, you need to get the bus to Ronda from the bus station discussed above. Please don't leave it to the day of the trip.
>>>>><<<<<

There is a significant problem with Ronda. Once you are there, you want to stay overnight for another day—lots of great places to have dinner and other sites to see.

>>>TIP<<<

If you plan to go to one of the beach resorts on the CDS from Seville, my strong recommendation is to spend the night in Ronda. Then, the next day board the other bus line "AVANZA" and head to Marbella, Fuengirola, or one of the other beach communities.

Coming from Seville, if you do not overnight in Ronda, it will be very difficult to travel on to the CDS communities with your bags late in the afternoon or early evening as you will have to find a place to stash them and perhaps your laptop. There are lockers at the bus station and train station in Ronda where you can lock your bags for the day. However, many times there are no vacant lockers, or the locks are broken. This is more the reason for staying overnight in Ronda.

If you care not to stay at the Parador, consider other hotels within walking distance to the Parador. On arrival in Ronda, your room may not be available. So, best to check your bags with the bellman.

If you are considering BlaBlaCar, ask your driver if he can "hang around" Ronda for several hours (with your bags in the trunk) and then take you over to CDS in the late afternoon. It will probably be the same amount of money had you stayed at a three-star hotel for the night and taken the bus over to one of the CDS communities the next day in the afternoon.

If you are not heading to CDS, then make sure you book your return bus to Seville. Also, bear in mind that if you visit CDS, you want to fly out of Malaga (AGP) instead of Seville or go back to Madrid. Best to consult the chapter "Malaga, Marbella and The Costa del Sol."
>>>>><<<<<

GIBRALTAR

No trip to CDS or Seville (it's a little more complicated) is complete without a day trip to the tiny country of Gibraltar, once a British Territory. It's the small piece of land, about three square miles at the bottom of the Iberian Peninsula, which is only nine miles across the Mediterranean Sea from North Africa.

The earliest inhabitants arrived about 50,000 years ago. The Rock has been there several million years.

First, it's been almost 300 years since the British claimed it (The Treaty of Utrecht), but Spain is still annoyed about the whole "takeover." No Spanish buses actually can get to Gibraltar, neither can taxis or trains. It's an odd thing, and you will probably not see this anywhere else in the world.

What you do, if you are not flying into Gibraltar (GIB), is that you must make your way to the small Spanish town of La Linea de la Concepcion (better known as just La Linea or "The Line") then walk through the gates to Gibraltar, and presto you are in one of the smallest countries in the world. More details later.

REMEMBER YOU MUST HAVE PASSPORTS!

GIBRALTAR WHAT TO SEE
First, this is another day trip which you should consider as an overnight trip. There are lots of modern hotels in Gibraltar and several in La Linea. If you are coming from Seville, consider departing Gibraltar (via La Linea) to one of the Costa Del Sol beach communities. It's only an hour away. So either pack your toothbrush and a change of clothing or pack your bags. In either case, it's kind of a drag (no pun intended) to carry your bags around all day while you shop. So best if you are going on to **CDS**, is to overnight at La Linea or Gibraltar, where you can stash your bags while you shop in Gibraltar and do some sightseeing.

>>>TIP<<<
If you are coming here to shop, be aware that many shops may be closed on Sundays. Best to check this out on www.visitgibraltar.gi
>>>>><<<<<

I have been to Gibraltar five times and always enjoy it. Imagine you come out of Spain and in a few minutes you are immersed in British culture. Red double-decker buses on all the roads (not a lot here). British stores for shopping like Marks and Spencer and dozens selling jewelry, clothing, cigars, liquor, and you name it. If you love shopping, this is the place.

Except for "The Rock," all the streets of Gibraltar are flat and easy to walk. I have often walked from Marks and Spencer back to the GIB airport, located at the entrance to Gibraltar, almost a half-mile away. It's only a 15-minute walk. However, if you are loaded with goods, it is best to take a taxi at a taxi stand or hotel back to the border.

>>>TIP<<<
If you are taking a bus back from La Linea, Spain, you must allow extra time after crossing the runway at the airport to clear customs. Sometimes there is a line (queue). Have your passports ready to cross back into La Linea, Spain.
>>>>><<<<<

If you are hungry when you arrive in Gibraltar, make your way to one of the many pubs and have some fish and chips, a meat pie or a burger and don't forget that "pynt" (sic) of warm ale or British beer. Okay, so much for the nourishment now on to the sites.

A visit to "The Rock" is always number one. There are three ways to visit this place. You can make your way to the cable cars and take them to the top of The Rock;

you can attempt to walk to the top. Yes, I said walk. However, I do not recommend it if you are out of shape. Many people take the cable car to the top and walk down. It's pretty safe, as you do walk on the side of the road opposing the traffic.

However, there is a far better way to visit The Rock and see the Town; and you can't beat it and the price!

>>>TIP<<<
After you enter Gibraltar, you walk across the runway at the airport (it's not a parking lot, it's an active runway). You will see anywhere from 3-8 white passenger vans at the round-about (the small circle) on the right-hand side. The drivers will "hawk" you for a tour of 90 minutes of The Rock and the Town. Now, get this, it's only 20 Euros a person. What a deal!

Once they get three or four couples (it takes about 10 minutes), they depart for The Rock. It's an excellent narrated tour of The Rock and the Town. After about 30 minutes, they will make a "facility" stop for the restrooms, the views, and a quick coffee break. They then continue to the top of The Rock for more views and pictures, another "facility" break, and a short narration of the tunnels and the Battle Galleries bored into the granite rock.

The best thing I always like about the top of The Rock are those monkeys. They are everywhere and will try to snag anything they can out of your hands. So try not to eat while you are at the top of The Rock, else the monkeys will have it for lunch. In addition, they even climb on top of the vans, and the drivers constantly chase them off with long sticks. You will laugh so hard; it will hurt! Also, don't attempt to "pet" the monkeys or befriend them. They do bite.

Upon coming down The Rock, the van returns to the town for a ten-minute overview. The place is so tiny you can't do a fifteen-minute tour of the city else you will be in the Mediterranean. The van will arrive on Main Street in the center of the Town. Note, they do not go back to the airport area.
>>>>><<<<<

>>>TIP<<
If you are planning to stay overnight and have your bags with you, you must first check into your hotel. A taxi will cost you less than five Euros to your hotel. Yes, they will take your Euros, no need to convert to English Pounds. Oh, did I mention you must drag those bags across the runway? Not a big deal. After check-in, have the hotel desk clerk call one of the vans, and they will swing around and pick you up. Yes, it's still only 20 Euros a person for a tour of The Rock and the Town.
>>>>><<<<<

If you are all shopped out or have a second day, the best is to explore the military side of Gibraltar in addition to the vast wildlife inhabitants of this small country.

If you are of the Jewish Persuasion, you will also find that Gibraltar has a large Jewish population (about 700), and would you believe they have four synagogues? You will discover several kosher bakeries and restaurants. Remember, most of them close early on Friday and are closed on Saturday for the Sabbath.

THE BASICS ON HOW TO GET TO GIBRALTAR
To reach Gibraltar, you take a bus to "La Linea de Conception." It's usually just referred to as "The Line" or just plain "La Linea." It is not an option to use public transportation from Seville to Gibraltar (La Linea). There are mountains in the way, and rail service is poor, and let's face it, do you want to be on a bus for four hours? If you want to visit Gibraltar for the day or, better overnight from Seville, it is best to use a car service known as www.blablacar.com. It's a two-hour run, and the price is only 12 Euros per person each way, assuming they will make the trip with four people.

>>>TIP<<<
If you are using BlaBlaCar, see if you can negotiate with the driver a day or two before what the charge would be if he/she hangs around La Linea for five hours. Essentially, you will be getting a private driver.

You can also query the internet for private hire for the day. However, I can tell you that it will probably cost you 200-300 Euros. If you can get two or four more people, you can split the cost. Most of the private cars out of Seville airport are available for private hire for the day. So best is to check private car service Seville Airport to Seville. Then email them for a quote for a day in Gibraltar. They will tell you they don't go to Gibraltar. Yes, we know that. Tell them La Linea.

I recommend leaving your hotel at 10 AM arriving in Gibraltar (at passport control) at 12:30 PM. Depart Gibraltar at 6 PM with a return to Seville at about 8:30 PM. Of course, if you are finished early and are shopped out at the end of the day, you can always text or call your driver to pick you up earlier at passport control on the Spanish side. Make sure you have international calling or texting to other countries as you will be using your smartphone in another country, i.e., Gibraltar. Check with your mobile carrier. If you are using a private car instead of BlaBlaCar it will probably be a high-end vehicle, i.e., Mercedes, BMW, etc.
>>>>><<<<<

If you are going by bus to La Linea, the bus will drop you off at the Autobus Estación in the center of town. You should note that the bus may stop before the central bus station. This is not the stop! You want the last stop. It is only a 10-minute walk (about 900 feet) to the entrance of Gibraltar from the central bus station. Remember to take your passports and use the facilities in the bus terminal or the McDonald's across from the entrance to Gibraltar (passport control in Spain).

THE DETAILS- TO GIBRALTAR FROM SEVILLE

First, if you are looking for bus schedules, do not, repeat do not, key in Seville to Gibraltar. You will not find any bus schedule. You need to take a bus to La Linea or "The Line" as they say.

The only affordable way (time and money-wise) to visit Gibraltar from Seville for the day or overnight is to use BlaBlaCar. If you take a bus via connections to La Linea, it will cost you about $40 and take you about four hours each way. You will find a one-day visit to Gibraltar far easier from one of the CDS communities, where it is usually only a one-hour trip from Marbella. So you may want to save this day trip for the CDS.

Because of the one-hour travel time from Marbella to La Linea, hiring a private car and driver will cost you a lot less than Seville, which involves a two-hour run each way. The best option is the bus.

THE DETAILS- CDS TO GIBRALTAR

If you are staying in Marbella, you will find over ten buses a day to La Linea. Don't be confused. Many buses take 15 minutes longer (normal from Marbella is one hour) because you need to change buses at the AVANZA hub station in San Pedro Alcantara. So, in summary, it takes about one hour fifteen minutes. The San Pedro hub is only about 6 miles past Puerto Banus Marbella. The fare is about $15 each way from Marbella to La Linea. Consult www.checkmybus.com or AVANZA.com.

La Linea is another one of those public transportation nightmares. If you are staying in Marbella, no problem. However, if staying in one of the beach communities toward Malaga, you will find it best to use www.blablacar.com or AVANZA (use the English version) or Busbud.com from the Fuengirola bus station about two blocks from the C1 line terminus.

>>>TIP<<<

On all three day trips described above, or "overnight and continue" trips, it is best to compare prices. In other words, if public transportation is $40 per person and you have four people in your party, it would be best to compare. So instead of $160 for bus tickets, BlaBlaCar may be only $15 per person.
>>>>><<<<<

>>>TIP<<<
Because of the COVID Pandemic, AVANZA has cut back bus service from Fuengirola (bus station) to La Linea. On arrival in the CDS area, have your concierge check the bus schedule, so you do not have to work your way to Marbella where there are about ten buses a day.
>>>>><<<<<

>>>TIP<<<
If you are using BlaBlaCar, see if you can negotiate with the driver a day or two before what the charge would be if he/she hangs around La Linea for five hours. Essentially, you will be getting a private driver.
>>>>><<<<<

TANGIER MOROCCO

Tangier is one of those places you can't get there from here. First, the two times I have been to Tangier (some times called Tangiers), Morocco, I went on a day trip with an outfit called "Tour Africa." They are no longer in business, but I understand there is another company offering a full-day tour out of the Costa del Sol beach communities. However, that being said, a visit to Tangier is truly an "experience."

First, as of this writing, all entry from Spain to Morocco is closed due to the COVID Pandemic. However, when this subsides, you can plan on a day, or better, an overnight trip to Morocco. I mean, let's face it, a day in

Morocco gives you the experience of visiting the Casbah, a camel ride, and buying a Moroccan rug.

To get there, you need to cross the straits of Gibraltar from the Spanish port city of Tarifa. There are two ferry companies, and there are about 12 crossings per day. The ferries also take cars and freight.

To get to Tarifa is an ordeal. First, awfully strange, Tarifa has no rail service. So, you must take a train from Seville to Cadiz or Algeciras. Then, you must take a bus (Transportes Generalis) to Tarifa. So just forget all those other ways of getting to Tarifa and follow this:

First consider, going to Tangier for an overnight trip. Or better taking the late ferry in the day back to Tarifa and overnighting there. There are lots of good hotels in Tarifa. If you want a "real" experience stay in Tangiers.

So here is how you do it --the easy way. There are two bus companies which offer direct service to Tarifa from Seville. The problem is that the bus leaves Seville at 6 AM and takes about three hours to reach Tarifa. At Tarifa, you board the ferry for that 90-minute ride across the Straits of Gibraltar. This is why I suggest an overnight trip with lodging, preferably in Tarifa, the night before you board the ferry. There are other ways to use Renfe and local buses. However, they come out to 4-6 hours to get to Tarifa from Seville.

Another approach when the COVID Pandemic is over and restrictions are lifted is taking one of the tour buses, which offer sightseeing and a lunch package.

If you are going on to one of the cities on the Costa del Sol, you will also find day packages to Tangier, Morocco. This is probably the best alternative.

SUMMARY ON THE THREE DAY TRIPS
If you have only one day extra for a day trip out of either Seville or CDS, my recommendation is by far "Ronda." Number two is Gibraltar, and last is a day or overnight trip to Morocco.

If you want to be creative, leave Seville for Ronda. Overnight in Ronda, continue to a CDS community, preferably Marbella. Why? Because I love Marbella. It's what I would call the Palm Beach of the area. It's got that class and style that the other communities just don't have. Marbella is difficult to describe. However, once at the CDS, you will know what I mean. You will find that Marbella offers excellent bus service to La Linea (Gibraltar) and other points in the area. So, treat yourself to a day trip. It's easy. And further, don't forget that great street market on Saturday at Puerto Banus.

Enjoy those day trips!

CHAPTER 12

THE NORTH
BILBAO-SAN SEBASTIAN
AND
SANTIAGO DE COMPOSTELA

ITINERARY "E"

INTRODUCTION

Till 1997 the draw of the Northeast, known as The Basque Country, and to the Northwest (Galicia) has been the resort city of San Sabastian (in the east) and Santiago de Compostela in the west. Along the Bay of Biscaye abutting the Atlantic, other well-known Spain cities such as Santander, Oviedo, and Gijon. These three cities are steeped in history.

Things changed in the mid-'90s when the Spanish and Basque Government invited the Guggenheim Foundation of New York to build a state-of-the-art museum of modern and Spanish art in Bilbao. The Guggenheim was opened in October 1997. The rest was history. It is now the number one "draw" to the area.

I can emphatically state that I was in the museum for about one hour and spent another three hours taking pictures of the exterior of this marvelous structure. It was designed by Frank Gehry, the 21st Century's most celebrated architect, in other words, the Frank Lloyd Wright of our day.

The building has a frame very much similar to the Statue of Liberty. Instead of being clad in copper, like the Statue of Liberty, it is covered with 60 tons of titanium steel sheets fabricated in Pittsburgh, Pennsylvania, and shipped to Bilbao, Spain for erection. The buildings and the complex sit on almost 700 pilings since the area was a wet marsh abutting the Nervion River. I would strongly suggest you take a look at the Guggenheim Bilbao Museum on the Internet and do make it a stop on your visit to Spain. Also, take a look at the photo on the rear cover with some modern artwork (sculpture) found at the Guggenheim. The area is served very well by Renfe.

Most people coming to this area are interested in just seeing one thing, the Guggenheim Museum. However, if you are of the Catholic Faith and are interested in visiting one of the Catholic shrines in the world, i.e., Fatima, Lourdes, etc., in that case, a visit to Santiago de Compostela is a must. However, bear in mind a rail journey to Santiago is a whole day, however, enjoyable.

QUICK FACTS- SANTIAGO DE COMPOSTELA

As stated before, this is one of the leading Catholic shrines in the world. St. James (the Great) is the patron saint of Spain. He was born and died (40AD) in Judea (now Israel and parts of the West Bank). The legend goes that he was brought back to Spain, and he was laid to rest in Santiago. Supposedly, a cathedral was built over the site of his remains.

Pilgrimages take place practically every year (it's a formula), and pilgrims walk hundreds of miles to reach the Cathedral of Saint James. The paths are marked for several hundred miles out of Santiago as the "Way of St. James." When they finally reach the Cathedral, they are awarded the "Compostela." It's an inscribed certificate attesting they made the walk.

I won't go into all the details of St. James; however, you can read them on the Internet. If you are a Catholic and have visited other shrines, i.e., such as Fatima, St. Joseph's Oratory, Lourdes, etc., visiting the Cathedral of St. James is a must.

>>>TIP<<<
Consider flying out of Santiago after completing your tour of the North of Spain. The process is similar to flying from Bilbao at the beginning or end of your Spain visit. Several major European airlines fly in and out of Santiago de Compostela (SCQ) from their hubs.

Flying out of SCQ eliminates the need to fly back to Madrid. Lufthansa is the most popular, with several flights to their Frankfurt hub, thus allowing easy connections to the USA's Lufthansa/United Airlines system to New York and Washington, their USA hubs.
>>>>><<<<<

HOW TO GET TO THE REGION
First, this region abutting the Bay of Biscaye comprises several what I call "sub-regions," the largest being Cantabria. Pretty much the entire area from Bilbao north (actually east) to San Sabastian and France is known as the "Basque Country." It is part Spanish and part French. Like, Barcelona with its Catalan Separatists, the people in this area who speak "Basque" have tried to form their own country from 1959 to 2018. In other words, break apart from Spain and France and call the place The State of Basque. In 2018, after years of terrorist incidents, the group known as the Basque Separatists finally gave up and dissolved.

Arriving in Bilbo, either by train or plane, is quite an experience. In the entire Basque region, you will see traffic signs and everything else in Spanish, English, and most importantly, in the Basque language, also known as "Euskera." The language is not a Latin or Romance-based language. It is the oldest language in Western Europe. Frankly, I don't even know where it originated; I don't think the Basque people know either. I call it "Jabberwocky."

For example, the word for thank you is "Scarry Cosco." Here is a sentence in Basque: Gizon-emakume guztiak aske jaiotzen dira, duintasun eta eskubide berberak dituztela; eta ezaguera eta kontzientzia dutenez gero, elkarren artean senide legez jokatu beharra dute. Don't even try to pronounce it! Translated into English, it means: "All men and women are born free, with equal dignity and rights; and since they have knowledge and conscience, they must act as legal relatives to each other" (from Google Translate). So much for the language of the Basque Country. Now on to Bilbao and the world-famous Guggenheim Museum.

>>>TIP<<<
If you consider originating your trip in Spain in either Madrid or Barcelona and going to Bilbao first, consider flying up there in about an hour. I tell you this because if you are either at **MAD** or **BCN** airports, all you need do is work your way over to the domestic terminal (not overseas where you probably arrived) and hop on the plane to Bilbao. If you want to do this, you need to buy your tickets to Bilbao (BIO) 6-8 weeks in advance.

In May of 2021, Air Europa has a 3PM flight from Madrid for about $60. If you are taking an overnight flight from the USA or Canada, consider a flight to

Bilbao (BIO) about 4-5 hours after you arrive in Madrid (MAD) or Barcelona (BCN). If you cannot get that Air Europa flight, most fares with Iberia hover around $110. Also, if you arrive at Terminal 4 in Madrid, it will take you about one hour to get through passport control and obtain your bags. You will then have to take the shuttle bus to the domestic terminal (usually terminal 3).
>>>>><<<<<

>>>TIP<<<
Here is another one of my tips for Bilbao. Consider taking the train up on your last day in Madrid. After visiting the Guggenheim Museum, fly out of Bilbao and connect in Madrid or Barcelona for your flight home. As a further tip, best to fly in and stay overnight at one of the airport hotels and fly out the next day, back to the USA or Canada. Don't chance the two flights for the same day. There is always less stress this way.
>>>>><<<<<

ITINERARY ROUGH OUT: A WEEK IN THE NORTH OF SPAIN-BILAO, SAN SEBASTIAN, AND SANTIAGO DE COMPOSTELA

Day 1- Train from Madrid to Bilbao
    See my TIP above about making Bilbao your first stop in Spain.
Day 2- The Guggenheim Museum in Bilbao
Day 3- A day in Bilbao/side trip to San Sebastian
Day 4- Rail Bilbao to Santiago de Compostela

Day 5- Santiago de Compostela
Day 6- Train back to Madrid
Day 7- Fly home from Madrid

>>>TIP<<<
VERY IMPORTANT- Check the Pilgrimage dates for Santiago de Compostela. You do not want to be in Santiago a week before or after a Pilgrimage. Trust me on this one. You will not find a hotel room for over 50 miles from Santiago. Secondly, you won't even be able to camp out in one of the parks.
>>>><<<<<

TRAIN- MADRID TO BILBAO
There are several trains a day to Bilbao. However, all of them require changes and take up to seven hours except the train late in the day. There is a direct train from Madrid-Chamartin taking about five hours and costing $30. If you want to change trains and take a few more hours to make the journey, it will cost you about $100. The only thing I can think of is that this is a "tourist" train or a mistake fare.

>>>TIP<<<
Make sure you arrive at Madrid-Chamartin at least 60-90 minutes before your actual departure. Under no circumstances should you "short" the time. You will need time to get some take-away food for the five-hour journey, and don't forget that bottle of water or wine

splits (with screw tops). Prices on the trains tend to be high, and not all trains have food carts or cafes on board. Also, like normal, you will have to clear security and have your ticket checked on the platform.
>>>>><<<<<

You should enjoy the scenery as it's a lovely train ride through the mountains and the hills north of Madrid on one of the high-speed Alvia (TGV type) trains.

You should note that Bilbao has two rail stations. They are adjacent to each other, just off the river. The Renfe trains from Madrid arrive at the rather large station, known as Bilbao-Abando. The station had a long name but has been shortened to just "Abando" for its host neighborhood. The other station next to Abando is known as "Concordia."

If you look at the map of Northern Spain, you will see many small and mostly seacoast cities, i.e., Santander, San Sebastian, Oviedo, Gijon, Maliano, etc., dotting the coast. Linking most of these small communities is a "narrow gauge" railroad line known as FEVE. This narrow-gauge railroad is now owned by Renfe and operated as Renfe-FEVE. However, since it is a different gauge, Renfe trains out of Madrid can't make a sharp turn out of, say Bilbao, and head over to Santander. It just won't work.

The Renfe trains out of Madrid run directly, in most cases, to these major cities, i.e., Bilbao, San Sebastian, Santander, and Santiago de Compostela (not on the FEVE rail system). So to get from one to the other, you have two choices. You can go back south to a connecting point on the Renfe network or take the FEVE train from one city to another. The only problem is that it does not go to Santiago de Compostela. See my directions on how to get to Santiago de Compostela below. It is a combination FEVE and a bus.

We are fortunate now since there is a high-speed rail link from Bilbao direct to Santiago de Compostela. Note, it does not go to the sea-side communities mentioned above. You would need to take the Renfe-FEVE railroad. As another option consider Renfe Bilbao to Leon and then Leon to Santiago.

There is no service on the Renfe-FEVE system from Bilbao east to San Sabastian to further add complications. That's another railway system known as "Euskotren." It does make a lot of stops. Once again, we are fortunate that many Renfe high-speed trains bound for San Sebastian may also stop at Bilbao.

I will discuss in depth how to get to San Sabastian and Santiago de Compostela from Bilbao. The best is to consult my map on the subject.

ON ARRIVAL AT BILBAO-ABANDO TERMINAL

When you arrive in Bilbao from Madrid, exit the train with the hordes of other tourists. I would guess most of them will be heading to hotels for an overnight stay before visiting this magnificent museum, or shall I say building. The train station is a short walk over to the museum. However, it is best to position yourself at a hotel on or near the beautiful riverfront in Bilbao which is in walking distance to the Guggenheim. These are all within walking distance from the Abando rail station. The ones which are a little longer will require a taxi, but in no case will it be more than 5-6 Euros.

You will need two or three nights in Bilbao. One, in the late afternoon, you arrive and the second after your visit to the Guggenheim. The next day you have the option of a day trip to the resort city of San Sabastian or traveling due west of Bilbao to Santiago de Compostela. On returning to Bilbao after visiting San Sabastian, you need to overnight and take the morning or noon train to Santiago de Compostela or fly out or rail back to Madrid if you are starting your visit to Spain.

These are the hotels within six blocks of the Bilbao-Abando rail terminal; all are 3 or 4 stars:
Sercotel Ayala (part of the Sercotel chain)
Sercotel Coliseo
Hotel Albando
Hotel Mercure Jardines de Albia (Accor Group Hotels)

These hotels I list by walking distance from the Bilbao-Abando rail terminal. They all have great views of the river and the city. When making reservations, do request a view of the river. Here is how you get there: Leave the station and walk to your right toward the river on the Hurtado de Amezaga Kalea; then cross the rotary and continue to the bridge over the river. If you are not too tired, pick up a few books on the massive outdoor bookstore just off the bridge rotary. Then continue on the Campo de Volantin Pasealekua (it parallels the river) until you find your hotel:

All below are three and four-star hotels on the river with a great view unless noted otherwise.
Hotel Bilbao Plaza (note it's a two star, but still fine)
Barcelo Bilbao Nervion
Hotel Conde Duque Bilbao
Hotel Hesperia (closest to the museum and my favorite hotel in Bilbao)

DAY 2- A MORNING AT THE GUGGENHEIM
On Day-2 of my rough out, arrive when the Guggenheim Museum opens. Consider having lunch at the café inside the museum or one of the abutting side streets. After the museum, nothing beats a walk on that boulevard facing the river. If you have not had a chance to check out the massive outdoor book market, now is your second chance. Hopefully, you can find a book in English left there by some of the "Brits".

DAY 3- A DAY TRIP TO SAN SEBASTIAN

There is a lot to see in this resort town. Very similar to Portofino in Italy. Lots and lots of shopping. Don't go on a Sunday, as many of the stores may be closed. I might add San Sebastian is very beautiful. It sort is from the late '30s in the art-deco period. You won't be able to do a lot in a day. It's a great walking city. However, you may want to spend an hour or two at the Aquarium and follow it up with an hour at the Primark.

Here is how you get there from Bilbao: First, San Sabastian (also known as Donostia) is about 60 miles due east of Bilbo and is served by another narrow gauge railroad Euskotren. It's quite modern, and there is a train every hour from Bilbao-Matiko station to Amara station in San Sabastian. The only problem is that the train makes about 40 stops and takes almost three hours to make the journey of that 60 miles. Do your best to take the bus, unless you enjoy a three hour train ride.

>>>TIP<<<
If you check the renfe.com schedule, you may be able to plan your day trip using the high-speed train. There are about four trains a day each way. I would suggest taking the train in the morning, do not purchase a round trip ticket. If you are still shopping, no problem as you can take the bus back anytime or the high-speed train if still available. However, check with Renfe since

even though the train operates over this route, they may not allow passengers to board at Bilbao.
>>>>><<<<<

There are several bus companies which make the run in a little over an hour. The bus company you want to use is "Lurraldebus" (www.lurraldebus.eus), specifically the U33 bus. Note like many buses for short-duration trips; there usually are no toilets. Other bus companies swing through Bilbao and head to San Sabastian once or three times a week, sought of like our Greyhound buses. The U33 (also known as DO-01, must be short for DOnostia) is the local bus in the area. It departs the bus terminal at Gurtyubay Kalea. Best to check with your hotel concierge or desk clerk the day before you make the trip. The fare is $15 each way. I might note that this bus also travels to and from the Bilbao (BIO) airport. So, if you arrive from Madrid or fly out from BIO, it is best to take this bus as they have frequent service to and from Bilbao airport.

>>>TIP<<<
If you have extra time, that same bus that will stop in San Sebastian goes on for about another 15 minutes to a medieval town on the French border known as Hondarribia. Shops also here, but not too touristy.
>>>>><<<<<

DAY 4 – TRAVEL RAIL FROM BILBAO TO SANTIAGO DE COMPOSTELLA VIA RENFE

The Renfe trains (Not Renfe FEVE) originate in San Sabastian about 60 miles due east. They stop in Bilbao to pick up passengers and continue their run through the northern part of Spain until they reach Santiago de Compostela. Depending on the stops made, you can figure 10-11 hours. It's a whole day's journey, but enjoyable because of the towns and the countryside traversed. You may have to connect on other times. As of May 2021 Renfe had the following schedule:

Lv Bilbao	Arv Santiago de Compostela		
9:20	19:35	$55	10h 15min
12:32	22.06	34	9h 34min

These are fast Long Distance (LD) Trains
They will do about 125 miles/hour
Make sure you bring some food and your water!

Santiago is not that large. The Cathedral of Santiago de Compostela is located in the center of the town. The rail station is located at about 6 PM, about one-half mile down from the Cathedral. So, you have two options, you can stay at a hotel within walking distance to the rail station, or you can stay closer to the Cathedral. If you are arriving hopefully by train, consider that you will be tired and want to plop in bed and get a good night's sleep. Best to just walk over to a hotel within 10 minutes of the rail station.

Here are the hotels within a few blocks of the rail station; all no more than a 10-minute walk:

Hotel Alda San Carlos
Tryp (it's the Spanish hotel chain) Santiago
Hotel Gelmirez

A 5 Euro taxi ride:
Eurostars Gran Hotel
Parador of Santiago de Compostela
(five stars and very historic, way to go for the experience.) Make sure you tell reservations you are a senior and do join "The Amigos Club".

If you are returning to Madrid, you will find high-speed rail service to Atocha and Chamartin stations. There are about six trains per day. Most of them are connections. The trains are fast, usually 4.5 to 5 hours for the journey. The cost is about $50.

Enjoy your time in Santiago de Compostela and your return to Madrid or fly back to the USA from SCQ (see discussion above).

CHAPTER 13

THE XYZ TOUR
ALSO KNOWN AS
"IF IT'S FRIDAY, IT'S GRANADA"

INTRODUCTION

Okay, now that you have read this book, you are probably thinking either of two things: a) I don't have the needed time to visit Spain or b) I don't have the money I need to visit Spain. It reminds me when I was in the escorted tour business. A travel agent would ask me to "trim the tour." So I would cut some days here and there. Then I would present it again, only to hear, "can you trim it more"? When I couldn't trim it anymore, I would tell the travel agent to rent a PBS program on Spain and show it to the group. I guess you get the point.

Anyway, here is a bare-bones rail itinerary of Spain, I call the XYZ Tour. It makes me dizzy just thinking about it. However, it may work for you. All you need to do is add a few days here and there. See my map in the rear of this book.

Here is the rough-out:
Day 1-   Overnight flight to Madrid
Day 2 – Arrive Madrid and sightseeing
Day 3- First train out of Madrid to Cordoba
          afternoon sightseeing
Day 4- Morning train Cordoba to Seville
          sightseeing Seville in the PM
Day 5- Morning train Seville to Granada
          sightseeing Granada in the PM
Day 6- Morning train Granada to Ronda
          sightseeing Ronda
I'm bushed and dizzy already
Day 7- Morning train Ronda to Barcelona
           via Malaga or Antequera. This is a real
           long haul. It probably will be the night when
           you arrive.
Day 8- Sightseeing in Barcelona
Day 9- Fly back to the USA or Canada

So what's missing?   First, there are **NO** day trips. Second, you will have to take an early morning train out of each city. Too bad you will miss that great Spanish breakfast and have to be content with a hard roll, butter and jam, and a coffee at the station.

What you won't see:
Toledo- Day trip Madrid
Segovia-Day trip Madrid
El Escorial and the Valley of the Fallen-

Avila- Day trip Madrid
Montserrat- Day trip Barcelona
Girona- Day trip Barcelona
Gibraltar and Tangier Morocco- Day trip CDS
and what about the entire Costa del Sol area?

On a positive note, you get to do a lot of napping on the train, especially on that Ronda to Barcelona long haul. You probably will have only about 4-6 hours to do any sightseeing. Remember, some sites like the Alhambra will take the entire day. You will have time to take a shower, a snooze, and go out to dinner before you retire, only to catch that first morning train out the next day.

If you want to do something like this, play around with the Renfe schedules and make your XY and Z, or should it be a start in Barcelona (instead of Madrid) with a direct high-speed train to Seville?

However, best to follow my day-by-day itineraries and enjoy Spain instead of rushing through it.

Anyway, it's just an idea. Now you can tell everyone you have been to Spain.

CHAPTER 14

LISBON...YES, IT'S PORTUGAL

INTRODUCTION

This chapter is about rail travel between Spain and Portugal, namely Lisbon. I include it because many escorted tours to the Iberian Peninsula include Portugal and Spain. Tour operators in the past package up Madrid, Andalusia (Seville, Cordoba, and Granada) with a return from Lisbon. Therefore, you may want to consider adding 3-5 days in Lisbon and the surroundings to your visit to Spain. Since the tour operators use coaches, it's easy to take the group from Seville to Lisbon. The trip with a tour coach runs about five hours with stops. On trips out of Madrid, coaches usually stop in historic Evora, Portugal, after traversing the Spanish countryside knowns as Extremadura. Now turning toward rail travel:

Because of the COVID-19 pandemic, as of this writing in May 2021 all rail travel between these two countries has ceased. However, when normalcy returns, here is what you probably will expect. I have modeled this after train routing before the COVID-19 pandemic.

Since I am addressing "rail touring," I will provide you with the connections from Madrid to Lisbon.

THE TRENHOTEL
Before the Pandemic of COVID-19, Renfe ran through service between Madrid and Lisbon every night. The train had rooms or what we call "Roomettes" on AMTRAK. It is doubtful if any service will resume.

YOU CAN'T GET THERE FROM HERE
Getting from Madrid to Lisbon by train is defined as one of those "You can't get there from here." Let me explain why. You can get a commuter train (Cercanias) from Madrid's Atocha station to the border town of Badajoz (Spain). From here you must take a bus for 2.5 hours to Lisbon. Not a big deal. However, the bus does not leave Badajoz until 2:45 PM. So, after you arrive in Badajoz you must overnight in a hotel since the train arrives several hours after 2:45PM. You are lucky since Badajoz is a very historic town.

The town, now a city, dates to about 4000BC. There are remnants of the old walls around the city. Best if you have time to start with a one-hour visit to the museum.

If you arrive on a Monday, there is a street market with several hundred stalls on Tuesday. Best to check the internet if they have they have changed the day. If you are considering purchasing any Spanish items to take home, this is the last place you will be able to do so.

For now, Renfe operates trains from Madrid to the border town of Badajoz, Spain. Because of COVID, there is only one train a day, leaving Madrid at about 4:38 PM arriving at about 9:46 PM. So best to figure about five hours. The nice thing about the trip is that it's only about $40. The train is a Cercanias (commuter) train. So don't expect one of those AVE 200 mile per hour jobs. However, the train does traverse the beautiful countryside of Extremadura at a speedy clip. Hopefully, in few years, there will be a high-speed rail link from Madrid to Lisbon. As of now, the Spanish and both Portuguese governments are working on the plan.

Once in Badajoz, you will find bus service directly to Lisbon several times a day from a few bus companies. However, you probably will be too bushed to go on a bus ride for 2.5-3 hours after a five hour train journey. So, enjoy your hotel night and a light snack in Badajoz.

Here are some of the hotels around the train station which are walkable. You can figure no more than 15 minutes. If your hotel is located in the city center, across the river, it is suggested that you take a taxi:

Hotels walkable are:
Mercure Badajoz (Accor hotel chain)
AC Hotel (a Marriott)
Sercotel

The bus will cost you about $25. There are two bus operators I know of: ALSA and the other is Flexibus. I would stay with ALSA since I believe they have four coaches a day from Badajoz to Lisbon. You should figure about three hours for the bus ride. Also, note there is a change in time since Portugal is on Greenwich time (same as London), and you will have to set your watch back one hour.

SEVILLE TO LISBON BY BUS, SORRY NO TRAIN
If you are in Seville and wishing to visit Lisbon and end your holiday there, consider taking the ALSA bus to Badajoz, spending the evening there, and then traveling the next day to Lisbon. You can take the bus also to Seville. However, it would be best if you connected with another ALSA bus in Badajoz. The connection may not work out; therefore, I recommend the overnight in Badajoz. In addition, that one-day journey from Seville to Lisbon will take an entire day. Best to figure about 8 hours. I have driven it in four hours. However, the bus does not go directly from Seville to Lisbon.

Make sure you do not pack your passports in your luggage bag. You may need them for inspection once in Portugal which is about 10 minutes out of Badajoz.

If you are considering flying between any Spanish airport, i.e., Barcelona, Seville, etc., and Lisbon, you will find that TAP (The Airline of Portugal) offers non-stop service several times a day. However, it is pricy compared to the train and the bus. If you figure the overnight stay at a hotel in Badajoz, the airline wins. They are about equal. Sorry, you will miss the site-seeing in Badajoz, the Tuesday street fair and that beautiful countryside of Extremadura.

Enjoy the sites of Lisbon: The Alfarma, St. Georges Castle, and day trips to Sintra and the ancient walled city of Obidos, which is a must.

If you are wondering how to get to Lisbon airport (LIS), we are now lucky since the Lisbon Metro now runs to the airport. A ticket will cost you about $2, and the express bus will cost you the same. Note, if you are taking a taxi, you can figure about $20. The airport is right outside the city. The best is to ask your hotel desk clerk or concierge, which is easier since the airport buses may stop only one block from your hotel instead of lugging that bag up and down the Metro stations.

Enjoy your flight home from Lisbon.

CHAPTER 15

THE FRENCH CONNECTION

INTRODUCTION
This chapter is about the high-speed rail service between Spain and France. It is not the 1971 film entitled "The French Connection" which won the best picture of the Academy Awards in 1971.

If you have ever been to the Venice Santa Lucia rail terminal, you will notice that there are Italian trains there and trains from all over Europe. You will see several Swiss Rail trains that started their journey from Zurich or Geneva and trains (DB Rail) from Germany. You may even see the Orient Simplon Express, which just arrived from an overnight trip from Paris.

This concept of direct trains to other countries from Spain started about ten years ago when Spain teamed up with France to run trains "straight through." What a great idea. Imagine, after visiting Barcelona the next day, you travel on a Renfe high-speed train directly into Paris. No need to change trains. The concept of linking two capital cities of Europe together is what

Renfe and SNCF (the railway company of France) proposed a little over ten years ago. Imagine boarding a high-speed train at Barcelona Sants and arriving in six hours 40 minutes in Paris Lyon station. This alliance between the two railroads is called ELIPSOS. The company is owned 50/50 by Renfe and SNCF.

COMPARISON FLYING VS. THE TRAIN
Spain's high-speed rail service to France originates at Barcelona Sants and in Paris terminates at Gare de Lyon. So no need to trek out to airports in either city. The journey takes only a little less than seven hours. By the time you pull out your laptop, have breakfast and lunch, and watch that beautiful countryside of Spain and France wiz by at almost 200 miles per hour, you arrive in Paris. If you do the math, it looks like this if you had to fly.

Leave Barcelona hotel for the airport: one hour
Check-in before the flight -------------------- two hours
Board the plane and prep for flight .5 hours
Flight time to Paris-------------------------- --two hours
Arrive Paris – reclaim baggage .5 hours
Taxi from any Paris airport to central Paris .75 min
Total time………………………………6.75 hours

If you took the high-speed train center city to center city, it would have taken 6 hours 41 minutes without "beating your gums out" with all that hassle. You don't have to sit in a cramped airline seat for two hours either. The AVE, TGV trains on this run are double-deckers.

>>>TIP<<<
You will find it best to ride on the upper level because of the excellent views of the Med and the mountains. You need to favor the right-hand side of the train (going forward) for the best views, Barcelona to Paris. You should favor the left hand-side, Paris to Barcelona.
>>>>><<<<<

Taking the train allows you more leisure time. You can edit those photos on your laptop, check your emails, etc. (the trains all have WIFI). Oh, I forgot to mention a leisurely breakfast (yes, you can bring your chocolate Croissants or Churros and a nice lunch (included in first class). If you are going Tourist class, make sure you bring your lunch, snacks and some water, and yes wine! There are plenty of "take-away" shops at Sants and Gare d Lyon in Paris. Don't forget that corkscrew and some plastic glasses. And most of all, you will be getting some rest as the world goes by; no rat race here.

Because of the COVID-19 Pandemic, the five trains in each direction have been cut back to only one per day.

As of May 2021, the AVE train for Paris leaves Sants station at 10:05 AM and arrives at Gare de Lyon at 4:46 PM. A Second (Tourist) class ticket will run about $122, while first class (meal and wine included) will cost you

$140. What a deal. Also, note you will not be able to use a Spain Eurail pass since this train is an inter-country train. You need an all Europe Eurail Pass.

On the return or, if you are originating your visit to Spain, the AVE train departs Paris at 10:14 AM, arriving in Barcelona at about 4:53 PM.   Second class runs about $90, and first class just a little higher.

I don't know why, but the trains from Paris to Barcelona cost less than the trains from Barcelona to Paris. In the future, look for other city pairs to be linked by direct train service. Perhaps we will soon see trains originating in Barcelona heading to Venice with stops in Marseilles, Nice, Monaco, and Genoa.

Enquire with Renfe or SNCF, as the Barcelona-Paris train does make limited stops in France i.e. Lyon, etc.

All said, this is an excellent way to travel relaxed and in comfort between these two capital cities. So, take out your laptop, do some work, read that book you started a week ago, grab a bite in the café coach, close your eyes and take a snooze. You will be in Paris (or Barcelona) in a few hours without all that running around and without all that stress.

CHAPTER 16

THE SPAIN EURAIL PASS & MORE

INTRODUCTION
So, you just came back from a dinner party with about sixteen friends and relatives, and you were telling them about your planned two-week rail trip to Spain next Spring. And, one of the guests at the party said: "Oh, you have to get a Eurail pass, it will save you money." Wrong! Here is what you need to know.

First, some definitions:
Eurail pass or Eurail Global pass is an inter-country rail pass. It can also be used for travel from one point in one country to another point in the same country. So if you are visiting Spain, you can travel from Paris to Madrid and then on to Barcelona.

The Spain Eurail pass, or the Renfe Eurail pass, the Renfe rail pass, etc., are all meant to be the same. All you need to know is that it is for travel within Spain. You cannot use it on the commuter lines in major cities or regions, i.e. C1, C2, etc. These are known as Cercanias lines. However, you can use the Cercanias trains three hours before your AVE train departs and four hours after your arrival with a Spain Eurail pass or a point-to-point ticket. The "free-ride" window varies by region. A little over an hour is allowed on the C1 line (CDS area) for trains in and out of Malaga Zambrano. Returning to the Eurail passes:

There are two types of Eurail passes. If you visit one country, i.e., Spain, you don't need a Eurail Global Pass. You need a Spain Eurail pass. Also, take note, if you are going on to Portugal or France and your journey begins in Spain, you will not be able to use your pass on the trip from Madrid to Lisbon or from Barcelona to Perpignan (France) and on to Paris.

Secondly, if you will be in Spain for two weeks, the pass does not give you unlimited travel on all the trains in Spain for those two weeks, hmmmm.

As of this writing, the smallest period is one month. However, you need not be in Spain for a month.
The Spain Renfe rail pass allows you options of travel:
4 days in one month
5 days in one month
6 days in one month

Thirdly, there are two types of passes. One is for first-class travel, and the other is for second-class travel. The first-class pass allows you to downgrade anytime to a second class (coach ticket). You cannot upgrade a second class rail pass by paying an upgrade or surcharge so you can ride in first class. And, finally, there are different age groups for the passes, i.e., Adult, Senior, Child, and family.

Also note, with most long-haul AVE and other high-speed type trains, you will have to make a seat reservation, either in first-class or second class. This is free on the Spain Eurail Pass. However, point-to-point tickets not using a Spain Pass will usually impose 10 Euros. This can be charged on your credit card.

As stated earlier in this book, most train operators, including Renfe operate using what is known as Dynamic Pricing. In other words, the closer you get to the train departure date, the higher the price will be. Dynamic Pricing is identical to the airlines in the USA. So, you may be paying $40 for that seat from Barcelona to Madrid, while the gentleman next to you may be paying $120 because he booked two days before and you booked two months before. So, in summary, as the train begins to fill up, the train operator increases the price on the remaining seats.

>>>TIP<<<
Once you determine your itinerary for your visit to Spain, you should determine if a Spain rail pass will pay off or should you purchase point-to-point tickets.
>>>>><<<<<

>>>TIP<<<

Absolutely, purchase your tickets directly from Renfe.com or OUIGO.com. Many "brokers" will add surcharges to the price.
>>>>><<<<<

>>>TIP<<<

The new **OUIGO** trains offered by the French railway are double-deckers. There is only one class of service, i.e., second (tourista) class (no first class). The seats are 20% smaller. They only allow one large bag and one carry-on bag. The positive point about the new French competitor is that they are about 50% less than Renfe. If you are on a very tight budget, you should consider this for your Madrid-Barcelona segments. It also makes justifying a Spain Renfe pass even more difficult. For now, **OUIGO** does not accept the Spain Renfe pass.
>>>>><<<<<

WILL A SPAIN RAIL PASS PAYOFF?

It's simple. All you need do is follow my rules:

First, determine if you want to go to first-class or second (Tourista) class. In the first-class coach, you will have fewer people. You will probably get a meal. It will be less quiet, and you probably won't have kids running around, and you will get a more comfortable and wider seat. To go first class of six days of travel will cost you $100 over a second class pass. In addition, at major stations, you get to plunk yourself in the first-class lounge (Sala Lounge), where you can enjoy snacks and beverages before your train departs. The Renfe Sala Lounge is very similar to the airline lounges. Once you have determined if you want to go, first-class or second class, you need to do the math.

Before doing the math, except for the Avila day trip, which is about two hours each way out of Madrid, you will find that it is not very cost-effective to use a day of travel on a 15 Euro day trip to Montserrat. If you simply take the cost of the pass and divide it by the number of days, it will give you the average cost per day. For example, if your rail pass costs $360 for travel for six days, technically, it costs you about $60 per day. You must also remember if you are arriving or departing on a reserved seat train, i.e., AVE type, you can use the commuter line (Cercanias or Rodalioes) trains for 90 minutes (varies by city). However, the price of a ride on most of these commuter trains is minimal compared to the long-haul AVE ticket. All you need do is wave your reserved seat ticket at the turn-style, and you will gain access to the commuter system in your arrival city. Now back to the math. To demonstrate this, I am going to use approximate round numbers:

Six days travel Spanish Renfe Pass (first-class) $360
Now, here is my itinerary with round trip (for your same-day trips) point-to-point pricing. It's from the A/B Itinerary Barcelona-Madrid:

Fly into Barcelona
  From Barcelona:
    Airport to the city- Rail passes not valid, cost $5
    Girona day trip R/T- $40 AVE
    Montserrat day trip – Cannot use pass (commuter train) R/T $24

Barcelona to Madrid- $90 AVE

From Madrid
    Toledo day trip- R/T $25 AVE
    Avila day trip- R/T $50 AVE
    Segovia day trip- R/T $72 AVE
    El Escorial day trip- Cannot use pass (commuter train) R/T $20

Madrid-Cordoba- $50 AVE
From Cordoba
  Granada day trip- $90 AVE

Cordoba to Seville- $40 AVE
Fly home from Seville

Total point-to-point AVE type valid for a rail pass: $457

Notes- You cannot use the commuter trains known as Cercanias trains or Rodalies in Barcelona with a rail pass. R/T means round-trip since this is a day excursion. However, once you exchange for a regular ticket, you can use the commuter rail system for 3 hours before and 3 hours after your inter-city AVE travel. Once again depends on the city or region.

In summary, since a rail pass is $360, you would think that since the AVE portion is $457, you would save money. FALSE! You can only use the pass for six days! So you need to pick the six highest dollar days to travel out of the eight described above:

    Girona day trip R/T- $40 AVE (no use)
    Barcelona to Madrid- $90 AVE Day 1 use it
    Toledo day trip- R/T $25 AVE (no use)
    Avila day trip- R/T $50 AVE   Day 2 use it
    Segovia day trip- R/T $72 AVE Day 3 use it
    Madrid-Cordoba- $50 Day 4
        Granada day trip- $90 AVE Day 5 use it
        Cordoba to Seville- $40 AVE Day 6 use it

The cost now for six days of travel totals $392 (a 6-Day first class rail pass would cost you only $360. So, you would be saving $32, hardly worth the effort in showing your rail pass and exchanging for the ticket. Yes, you will have to wait in line and arrive an extra 15 minutes early to show your pass and get a ticket.

>>>TIP<<<
While I used an "average" trip cost from Renfe, bear in mind that many trains outside of the morning and evening hours (rush hours, which are often commuters

to work, i.e., Segovia to Madrid) most of the trains from 9:30 AM- 3:30 PM are less money.
>>>>><<<<<

>>>TIP<<<
The best approach is to pick the trains first. Then perform the cost analysis. For example, if you want the 9:30 AM train from Barcelona to Madrid and it's $90, use this in your calculations even though mid-day trains may be less. And, remember, once you pick them, say 45 days prior, you must make a reservation and get a seat number on purchasing.

You still have to show your rail pass at the check-in counter and exchange it for a confirmed ticket with a coach and seat number. You don't board a train and flash your rail pass in front of the ticket collector!
>>>>><<<<<

In summary, unless you are doing real "long-hauls," the Spain rail pass won't pay off. Yes, if it were a true Eurail pass, i.e., country to country, it usually does pay off, i.e., Paris to Madrid, Madrid to Rome, Rome to Athens, etc. It's simple; some countries are not geographically large enough to justify an "in-country" rail pass. This is true for Italy, Spain and others.

Here is where the Spain rail pass would payoff:

Arrive Barcelona, after several days in Barcelona-
Then rail, day journey's (one way):
Barcelona to Seville rail day 1- $100
Seville to Bilbao day rail 2   - $130
Bilbao to Santiago de Compostela rail day 3- $50
Santiago de Compostela to Madrid rail day 4- $100

Fly home from Madrid-

Total point to point- $380
4-day rail pass would be $312

Of course, if you pick your trains by the time of day, the point to point may drop severely. Also, some trains do not offer first class!

Also, a 10% senior discount (over 60) will not earn you anything since point-point fares will also give you a 10% discount.   In simplicity, it makes the difference of point-point vs. the Spain rail pass even less attractive.

If you are traveling with a family, you also need to run the numbers for a Spain Renfe pass for the family. The best approach is to contact Renfe.

CHAPTER 17

MONEY, CREDIT CARDS, TELEPHONES, INSURANCE, HOW TO PACK, AND SECURITY

MONEY

I have always found it far better to get my Euros out of an ATM than my local bank and obtain them. As discussed in an earlier chapter, you should avoid going over to any of those money changers at Madrid or Barcelona airport. These airport money changes, and the ones you will find on the Gran Via in Madrid define the phrase "what is a ripoff."

The first rule, do not visit your local bank. That's another ripoff; surcharges and the worst rates. Second, realize that if you arrive at **BCN** or **MAD** airports, you won't need Euros since all forms of public transportation will take your credit cards. However, that being said, if you insist on a few Euros when you arrive in Spain, here is what you need to do:

After you clear Spanish passport control and hopefully stamp your passport, you need to work your way to the baggage claim area. Retrieve your bags and follow the green arrows or green lights over the exit doors. They are marked "Nothing to Declare." Once you are out of the "controlled area," you need to locate the ATM. These are often called in Europe "Cash Points." The best approach is to locate a sign. If you cannot, it is best to ask someone of authority. Many times when you exit the controlled area, you will find a police officer. Sometimes, I walk up to a concession where they sell coffee, etc., and ask a person. You can also ask one of the rental car clerks. You have it made if you are being picked up by a private car and driver. In this case, the driver will escort you over to the cash point.

What's important here is that the ATM be a "bank ATM." In other words, it will bear identification like Banco Santander, BBVA, etc. Before you leave the USA or Canada, make sure you inform your bank that you will visit Spain and use their ATM system.

It's best to always get the maximum amount. On most withdrawals, the local bank in Spain will only allow about 300 or 250 Euros a day, even though you may have set a far higher limit with your local bank.

Transaction fees vary by the US banks. Many US banks have reciprocal agreements with banks in Spain, where the US bank waives the foreign transaction fee. The US megabanks, i.e., Bank America, Chase, etc., have deals with banks in Spain to waive their fees. Best to contact your bank. However, this may require you to go hunt down one of those "mutual" ATMs.

If you compute the fees, you don't want to get 100 or 200 Euros. You will pay a local bank fee and a domestic fee in addition to the exchange rate. So if those two fees add up to $12, you will be paying 6% ($12 per hundred) on 200 Euros before you even consider the exchange rate. So in simplicity, get the most the machine will give you. Also, each additional day you can "hit" another ATM to take out more Euros.

Don't get worried if you have too many Euros in your wallet at the end of your trip. You can always pay your last hotel bill partly in Euros and partly by credit card.

How many Euros do you need for a week? First, it's best to charge everything on your credit cards and only use cash for small items, i.e., taxi cabs (many now take credit cards), tips, souvenirs, street market items, and cafes. As a rule of thumb, I figure about 300 Euros a week for a couple. Spending this amount of money may probably be on the high side. It all depends on how much shopping you do, how many times a day you swing into a café or a stand-up bar and have a café and a snack. Most of these places will prefer to take your Euros in place of a credit card, making you look foolish. I prefer to charge all restaurants and hotels with my credit cards. There is a lot of security here since your credit card never leaves your hands, unlike the USA.

>>>TIP<<<

It is best to keep the bulk of your Euros in a money belt and not in your pocket or your wallet. Spain is a very safe country; however, it is just traveler savvy. So, after I get my Euros, I go back to my hotel room and stash them in my money belt or my money pouch that fits around my waist directly *under* my pants. This technique works primarily for women since it is challenging to wear a money belt. Don't mess around at the ATM trying to stuff your Euros in your wallet.
>>>>><<<<<

>>>TIP<<<

If you are visiting an ATM, do not make that visit after dark. Also, have someone escort you and do make sure no suspicious characters are hanging around. Best to visit the ATMs located in the lobby of the bank.
>>>>><<<<<

And one more point. Traveler's checks are usually not accepted anymore. If you can convince your hotel to take a few traveler's checks, they will probably charge you an additional 5%. However, now in the age of credit cards, they are a thing of the past.

CREDIT CARDS

Like using ATM bank cards, you should inform your credit card companies that you will be in Spain for a specific time frame. Most establishments usually take VISA and Mastercard. Because of the higher commission fees involved, many establishments will not accept American Express. However, most hotels three-star and above will. I find it always best to take two cards (or better three) with me. You never know when that chip or magnetic strip will stop functioning.

It is best to use a credit card where there are no foreign transaction fees. Many credit card companies convert the Euros on your transaction to the rock bottom bank exchange rate. However, they may add a 3% foreign transaction fee for no reason whatsoever. It is best to obtain credit cards which do not carry any foreign fees.

If you have a bank debit card, you will find that all of the above transactions you can do with a credit card you can also do with your debit card. Just make sure you have enough funds in your bank account before you leave home. Suggest you contact your bank before leaving the USA or Canada to obtain another bank card just in case your chip or magnetic strip is worn. Being in Spain is one place you don't want to pay $200 for an overnight FedEx for a replacement bank card.

Also, if you are interested in obtaining free airline points, hotel points, or gift points, you ought to consider getting a points-based credit card. Just for obtaining the card, the issuer usually will give you anywhere from 20,000-80,000 points for spending $1000 to $3000 on the card in the first, say 90 days; what a deal. It is best to check out the website *thepointguy.com* for an analysis of the offers.

And one more thing to consider: Many establishments, not just in Spain, but worldwide, will ask you sometimes on a Visa, Mastercard, or other charge card transaction if you would like to pay in Euros or US dollars. The answer to this is to ALWAYS pay in Euros. When you offer to pay in US dollars, they will be giving you THEIR exchange rate. This is usually not the bank exchange rate. It's almost identical to paying in dollars at the hotel when you check out. They will usually have a sign posted with THEIR popular exchange rates. If the current bank exchange rate of Dollars to the Euro is $1.22, expect them to have you give up $1.44 for each Euro to pay your bill. Same with the credit card choice.

TELEPHONES

Because of new technologies developed in the past five years, there are now many more ways to make telephone calls back to the USA and even local calls.

So let me go over the popular alternatives. Most of you are quite familiar with them because of their use in the COVID-19 pandemic time frame.

>>>TIP<<<
Except for a local, 800, or 900 call, try not to make any calls from your hotel room and charge it to your room bill. The hotel will usually charge you a flat rate of at least one Euro for each call. You will find that the rates charged will be astronomical when calling back to the USA or, in fact, other points in Spain. It is best to check first with the front desk before any surprises about a ten-minute call back to the USA for a whopping $79.
>>>>><<<<<

TELEPHONE TRAVEL PLANS
Many national cell phone providers, i.e., AT&T, Metro PCS, and Verizon offer foreign travel plans for traveling abroad. They usually give you a package plan, but after those usually 100 minutes per month expire, they charge you about $.35 per minute to call the USA and receive calls from the USA. Without any plan, figure about $1.75/minute to call the USA from your mobile.

The travel plans also offer a small about of data allowance and text messages. For example, Verizon offers 500 Megabytes per month and about 100 sent text messages on its monthly travel plan in addition to 100 minutes of in/out calling. As of this writing, the

Verizon plan discussed is about $70/month per phone (line). Other plans are available. The allowance of 500 Megabytes does not go far. You will undoubtedly use this up very quickly if you are transmitting photos of your vacation or viewing your Facebook account without the use of WIFI or any other form of direct internet access. And if you would like to chat outside of a WIFI area, it will cost you $.35 per minute after the 100 minutes are up. If you do the math, that's $21/hour.

If you are not using WIFI from your hotel room and are using the cell phone system, i.e., 4G or 5G, expect a jumbo cell phone bill when you get back to the USA. Contact your cell phone provider for more information and discuss a travel plan to use your cell phone in Spain outside of a WIFI area. Better it would be if you just used WIFI and turned your cell phone radio off. Check your settings, or better call your cell service provider.

As discussed earlier, there are several alternatives to travel plans. Here are several of them if you must use your cell phone when not in a WIFI area.

SPANISH CELL PHONE
If you will be in Spain for a minimum of 10 days and you need to be accessible 24/7, it may prove beneficial to obtain a Spanish cell phone. For as little as $50, you can purchase a Spanish cell phone with a SIM card. No, it won't be an iPhone, but it may be a basic

Android-type phone. The SIM card in your Spanish phone will determine your carrier and your phone number. You can recharge the phone at numerous locations, including many ATMs described above.

Four of the largest providers are Yoigo, Movistar, Vodafone, and Orange. Rates are much less expensive for calling back to the USA. Best to stop into a cellular store and check the rates before you purchase. Also, the phone comes in handy when you have to call a restaurant or your hotel. They are quite simple to use with just a few Spanish words, which you can figure out in minutes. Many will allow English as the language of choice. It's a small investment if you are running a business or just have to get that call from a loved one on the streets of Cordoba or elsewhere.

TELEPHONE CARDS

This is an easy one. You purchase a ten Euro phone card at your local tobacco shop or anywhere they are sold. You then dial an 800 number (toll-free from any phone), you key in your card number, and then the phone number you wish, and presto, the call is made. This costs far less than the travel plans offered by the US cell phone service providers. It is not necessary to deposit any coins in a payphone (coin phone) to dial an 800 number. However, it is best to keep a Euro in your pocket if needed. It will be returned after you dial the 800 number. Many payphones do not require any deposit. Just pick up the handset and dial. Also, bear in mind that sometimes hotels do charge to make an 800 call which defeats the purpose of using a telephone calling card. Best to use a public coin (or card) phone.

GOOGLE PHONE/ SKYPE/ FACETIME

New internet technologies have emerged in the last five years, allowing us to use WIFI internet access to bypass the local telephone companies most of the time. There is no charge for obtaining a Google phone number, sometimes called Google Voice. It's a regular American telephone number complete with an area code. However, you need to originate the call only when you are connected to the internet, usually via WIFI. If you call another person connected to the internet, the call will go through with no problem over the internet and bypass the telephone system completely. However, if you are going "off-net," i.e., the other phone is not connected to the internet, i.e., it's a landline or a cell phone, you may to pay a small connection charge which amounts to about 1-2 cents a minute. This is because Google has to "dump" the call into the public telephone system. So, to do off-net calling on a Google number, you will need to charge your account for at least $10 or $20. The funds don't expire, and you can even use them in the USA. You must also download the Google Voice App on your cell phone, tablet or PC. And yes, to re-iterate, you must have WIFI.

In summary, what I usually do while in Spain is use my Google number first, if that has a problem (lower bandwidth) I make my call on my Spanish cell phone or my American cell phone using my travel plan.

Skype and FaceTime (FaceTime is a trademark of Apple, Inc.) also can be used, but unlike the Google number, they only can provide WIFI or internet calling to internet calling. So both the originating iPhone or Apple device or a tablet must be connected to the internet and the receiving device. You can't go off-net. Sorry, no support on Android or Windows devices.

Also, beware that many larger hotels restrict high bandwidth applications from hogging their pipeline to the internet. Running FaceTime or Skype may slow down other applications being run by other guests, e.g., checking their emails at the hotel, so you will not be able to connect via these WIFI/internet technologies.

Facebook, Inc. launched "Messenger" several years ago. You need not belong to Facebook to use it. Also, the Messenger app runs on iPhone, Android, and some desktop apps. Messenger allows WIFI to WIFI calling, live video, and other real-time apps, and it's free.

MEDICAL INSURANCE
Seniors who have their medical insurance with Medicare are **NOT** covered while out of the country. If

you have a supplement, they usually will not pay anything unless Medicare pays first. So you need some type of medical insurance. It is best to check online or with your present insurance carrier if not Medicare. Make sure the insurance coverage includes accident and sickness. Some of these travel insurance providers are *insuremytrip.com*, *travelguard.com*, and *allianztravelinsurance.com*. Also, do check with your local insurance agent and do compare rates.

You can also purchase a yearly policy that will cover you if you are frequently out of the country. Make sure the provider will also cover your traveling partner if you are forced to come home early.

Also, remember that Spain is a first-class modern country, and they will provide you with medical attention equal to or better than what you would expect to receive in the USA.

HOW TO PACK

You must pack a little differently for a rail trip than you would for an escorted tour. First, I recommend a piece of luggage that is lightweight and has wheels on it. The piece of luggage should not weigh a lot. It should be no more than 24 inches in length and no more than 14 inches in height and width. If it has one of those pull-out handles, the more, the better. And do consider some of the new bags with lots of those outside pockets.

Now, what to pack? First of all, you will need a comfortable pair of walking shoes or sneakers. Do not try to "break-in" a pair of shoes or sneakers on a trip— a bad idea. Ladies, do not bring an extra pair of shoes, and do leave those high heels home. I usually suggest only one pair of shoes, the ones you wear. Every time I take a dressy pair of shoes to wear to a nice place for dinner, I find that everyone else is wearing sneakers.

Spain is laid-back; however, they will get dressed up for a nice Sunday afternoon dinner. So, guys, you will have to take the T-shirt off and put on something more "dressy-casual," like a shirt with buttons.

The whole concept in packing is to pack light. We use lots of large one-gallon zip lock bags so we can see everything we pack. If you are on your trip for more than 12 days, consider that you may have to spend a few hours in a laundromat. Best to do laundry one evening on the Costa del Sol. Lots and lots of laundromats only a few blocks from your hotel. It's no big deal to spend a few hours one evening doing your laundry. You may learn some Spanish if you decide to hang around the laundromat reading *El Mundo* with the locals. If you don't want to be bothered, ask the concierge at your hotel and pay the $12 to have your underwear laundered and returned to your room.

After you are fully packed, remember this—You will only wear about 50-70% of the items in your bag. So un-pack it all and say to yourself, "what can I do without"? Remember that you can always buy that nice shirt at the Saturday street market in Madrid or Marbella. So, you need to allow space to bring home all those souvenirs you buy. So make sure you are no more than 30-35 pounds in each bag. Most airlines allow 23kg per bag (50 pounds). Since you are on a rail tour, you will only be taking one large bag and a carry-on.

It is best to take only one carry-on bag for two people. Sometimes you can avoid this completely and stay with your two pieces of luggage (per couple) and pack any carry-on stuff in a lightweight carry bag, which you pack in one of those two big bags. It's just easier for rail travel. Do pack your medications in your carry-on bag. We also pack a lightweight "day" bag. I carry it on my shoulder with my books and maps, and of course, my tickets and other travel documents. And do carry your passports on your person and not in any bag.

SECURITY

There are very few violent crimes committed in Spain. Few people, if any, have guns. If you watch TV at night, you will usually see game shows, soccer, or dance/music entertainment programs which are very much like "Sabado Gigante" which appears on Univision every week. You won't see TV programs that feature any type of violence except perhaps a re-run of an American western featuring John Wayne. Violent crime is pretty much non-existent in Spain. However, Spain and many European countries make up for this in what is known as petty crime. Petty crime is basically "pickpocketing" and other devious means to make you part with your wallet, passport, jewelry, or your laptop, or something else.

I shouldn't single out Spain. It is just a common "nuisance" in most European countries and, in fact, all over the world but pretty much non-existent in America except on New Year's Eve in Times Square. Read the following tips and be "Street Savvy":

TRY NOT TO STAND OUT AS A TOURIST

The more you try to look like a local, the better it will be. For men, leave that sport jacket home and forget those expensive pair of trousers and that elegant-looking shirt. Instead, wear a pair of blue jeans or khaki pants, better if they are khaki cargo pants. For women, best to wear Capri's and avoid fancy-looking dresses or even sundresses. For shoes, wear comfortable sneakers or walking shoes. And if you are there on your honeymoon, don't dress for it. It is far better to dress down; else, you will appear as a target for pickpockets and scammers. In other words, DON'T FLASH.

DON'T DRESS LIKE AN AMERICAN

First, leave those ball caps and T-shirts that are truly American home. If it says "HARVARD" or the ball cap says "RED SOX," leave it home. And, don't, repeat, don't wear that sweatshirt which says **SPAIN** on it. Just pack that sweatshirt up and take it home.

>>>TIP<<<
Never take anything on a trip that you can't afford to part with, including your tablet or laptop.
>>>>><<<<<

To this day, I do not bring my tablet or my laptop with me, only a smartphone. If I need to use a computer to send an elaborate email or a document, I find that most hotels either have a business center machine or will allow you to use one of their computers. If all else fails, I hunt down an internet café and invest 3-5 Euros to use their machine for an hour. This way, I have less stress on someone removing my laptop from my hotel room.

>>>TIP<<<
Ladies leave your good jewelry, and men leave that Rolex home! I have heard too many stories and have read too many reviews, where a couple goes to breakfast in the hotel, the woman leaves that beautiful "cocktail" ring on the night table only to come back from breakfast and find it missing. It is best to leave your fine jewelry home and take no jewelry at all. If

you must wear a watch, take an inexpensive watch that you can afford to part with; or, better buy one in Spain.
>>>>><<<<<

>>>TIP<<<
Remember to take your wallet and your smartphone with you to breakfast. Don't assume that everyone in the hotel is honest. Most of the time, they are, and minor crimes are usually not committed by the hotel staff, but by others.
>>>>><<<<<

Don't be alarmed that on check-in at your hotel, you must surrender your passport. The desk person will give it back to you once they make a copy. You should request it back the next day or before you depart.

Many older European hotels require you to drop off your room key at the front desk when leaving the hotel. Do not leave it on top of the counter so anyone can pick it up and use it. Give it to the front desk person or place it on the other side of the counter and not on top.

AVOIDING PICKPOCKETS
First, realize that most pickpockets are looking for your money, then your passport, and then your credit cards. All of them have some value.

>>>TIP<<<

So for the money, you need a money belt or a money pouch. I recommend the money belt available from Amazon B015HXS2QS; about $10. You can easily fold six 100 Euro notes or six 50 Euro notes into the belt. You can also use an undergarment money pouch. However, if you are wearing one, make sure you use one of those large safety pins to pin it to your underwear; look at Amazon B01G1ORT5M. This money pouch also adds RFID protection. The only problem with this money pouch is that when you go to the bathroom (and yes for women and men), it becomes somewhat of a hassle to unpin it and pin it back.
>>>>><<<<<

>>>TIP<<<

Men should carry a sacrificial wallet in their back pocket. Never carry your real wallet in your back pocket. I carry two wallets with me. One is my regular wallet which I keep my hand on in my front pocket, and the other is my SACRIFICIAL WALLET which I keep in my back pocket. However, most of the time, I wear those "cargo" pants, so I don't have to keep my hand in my pocket. See my TIP on cargo pants and pockets.

Many years ago, I asked my very wise father why he carried two wallets. He lived in New York City. He said, "Bob, you see this wallet. I carry it in my back pocket. If they want to mug me or pick my pockct, they

256

get the sacrificial wallet". I asked him, what's in the sacrificial wallet? He said, "all they will find is five dollars and some garbage receipts and some crappy discount cards you get in the mail that look like credit cards. So, if they picked my pocket and ran down the street, it wasn't a big deal. What a surprise they had, no-hit at all, the muggers got nada!"
>>>>><<<<<

>>>TIP<<<
If you can, men wear those cargo pants and make it difficult for a pocket picker to remove anything without a struggle. Don't put anything of value in the type of pocket you need to zip up; you need to use those cargo pockets with buttons on them, not zippers. This is an easy one. However, it just makes it more challenging to get anything out of those pockets once you put buttons on them. Pickpockets want to "hit" the victim and run; they won't hassle with buttons. You can also take those pants to a tailor and just tell him/her to add two buttons to each of those zipper pockets. It will cost you a big $5-10 per pair of pants. Money well spent.
>>>>><<<<<

>>>TIP>>>
If possible, wear a jacket with inside pockets with zippers. This is for the gents and the ladies. This affords the best protection for your wallet and passport. You

can also use one of those travel vests. However, make sure it has inside pockets.
>>>>><<<<<

>>>TIP<<<
In most European countries, men have handbags just like the ladies. You will find it an excellent means to carry your wallet, keys, smartphone, maps, and all those good things. However, you must have one with a strap that will go over and across your shoulder. Make sure the flap is turned inward so it can't be easily opened.
>>>>><<<<<

>>>TIP<<<
Now for the ladies: Just like the men's bags, you need to have a large handbag with a strap which you carry over and across your shoulder. Do not take your regular handbag as it can easily be torn from you, i.e., "snatched." Also, remember to put your wallet back in your bag. Don't just drop it in without re-zippering.
>>>>><<<<<

>>>TIP<<<
This tip is for single young women and guys who like to wear backpacks, sometimes called rucksacks. You are at a major tourist attraction or using the subway, and you are at a standstill. The person behind you zips open the small compartment on the top of your backpack, and presto, your passport is gone. The

advice here is don't put anything but tissues or napkins in these compartments. All your valuables should be in the main compartment of your backpack, where the zipper is inaccessible unless you remove the entire backpack from your body.
>>>>><<<<<

>>>TIP<<<
If you are the type of person, who likes to wear one of those fanny packs, **DON'T** wear it on your hip or your fanny. Instead, you should wear it in front of you. If you are taking the Metro in Madrid or Barcelona, this is extra important since at rush hour, trains may be packed, and it is easy to remove it on your side.
>>>>><<<<<

>>>TIP<<<
Most pickpockets use the distraction technique. They operate in teams or simple pairs. One of them distracts you while the other lifts your wallet or whatever. All you need to remember here is to keep your guard up and do not get distracted. Don't bend over if someone drops some coins or jewelry. It's a ploy. Let them pick it up.
>>>>><<<<<

>>>TIP<<<
Never ask a single person to take your picture. This is a bad idea, even if it's a single woman that looks nice and sweet... it's a setup. You think they are tourists.

Nope, they are part of the team! She may take your picture then get bumped by her "partner," who will run off with your new iPhone. Of course, she will say, "I am sooooooo sorry!" It was all a ploy or a good act. If you need someone to take your picture best approach is to spot another tourist COUPLE, policemen, or a shopkeeper who will take your picture. I can assure you none of these people will run with your smartphone.
>>>>><<<<<

>>>TIP<<<
Avoid "hit 'em and run" ploys. When walking on the sidewalk, do not walk close to the curb; instead, walk on the side away from the curb. Ladies should hold their handbag over their shoulder, such that the bag is away from the curb. If you walk close to the curb, you risk the person on the motor scooter grabbing your bag.
>>>>><<<<<

>>>TIP<<<
If you are taking the Barcelona or Madrid Metro, be extra cautious and avoid being the last one in the subway car. Pickpockets often can push you in, and as they do this, you will part with your wallet or handbag as they run out of the station when your train pulls away. In other words, you will be on the moving train, and they will be on the platform waving at you! Just wait till they open up that sacrificial wallet.
>>>>><<<<<

>>>TIP<<<

If you need to take out a tour book or a map and someone approaches you to help you, say, "no thanks, all set." Avoid open spaces when opening up a map or a tour book. It is best to back up against a building where no one can come up from behind you.
>>>>><<<<<

>>>TIP<<<

Make photocopies of all your credit cards and passports and keep them in a separate place. You can also take photos of them and keep them on your smartphone (assuming they haven't taken your smartphone). If you need to get replacement passports, the American or Canadian Embassy in Madrid can help you. If you are in other cities, you will usually find an American or Canadian consulate. Make sure you bring your passport copies, this will ensure rapid replacements.
>>>>><<<<<

>>>TIP>>>

In addition to pickpockets, be on the lookout for scammers. Here is how to avoid them. There may be persons roaming around one of the Gaudi houses or the Mezquita in Cordoba who will offer you a tour. They pretend to be licensed tour guides. They will be wearing badges that even look official. You see an extensive line waiting for tickets. The scammer approaches you and your girlfriend and says, "Ladies,

I can take you on a 40-minute tour for only 20 Euros, and I can also whiz you through the security line with my official badge". After you accept his offer and pay him the 20 Euros, he will disappear into the security line, and you will never see him again.

>>>>><<<<<

There are lots of other scams which are quite complex. Suffice it to be, that if the offer is too good to be true, it's probably not true. So, just keep on walking.

Here are some final thoughts on security. If anything is missing or stolen of real value, you should visit the local police department and file a report. Obtain a copy of the report of your filing, even if it's in Spanish. For insurance purposes, make sure you tell the police exactly what was taken. You probably will not get that cocktail ring back. Still, your insurance company may provide a replacement if you have it listed on your jewelry schedule of your homeowner's policy (or HO6 policy if you have a rented apartment or home). If you cannot produce a police report, you are out of luck, and usually, no replacement will be granted. I thought I suggested in a tip to leave that $3,000 ring home?

In summary, Spain is quite safe but, there are always those that will attempt petty crime. The best defense is to be vigilant all the time. Do not get distracted or enter into a potential "setup." Keep your bags zipped (even in the hotel room) and heed the points I raised. You may want to re-read them on arrival in Spain.

IN SUMMARY

I do hope you enjoyed this book. As stated in the introduction, it is not an entire travel guide to seeing Spain via train. It is intended to provide a day-by-day itinerary for seniors, and in fact, everyone, to visit the highlights of Spain without having to spend an awful lot of money on an escorted tour.

So do enjoy this beautiful country of Spain, admire those magnificent Medieval castles and cities and think of the days when Don Quixote, Sancho Panza and their trusted horse Rocinante traveled the roads of Spain.

You can travel those same roads. Sit back and relax and enjoy Spain by rail. I wish you well, and thank you for reading this book.

Bob Kaufman, The Author

APPENDIX A

BARCELONA HOTELS RAMBLAS AREA

Continental Palacete – 3 blocks west of PC
Atlantis- 2 blocks south of PC
H10 Raco Del Pi- 3 blocks off Ramblas
Continental Barcelona- on Ramblas
El Avenida Palace- 4 star one block west of PC
Lleo- 2 blocks south of PC
Cataluna Plaza- 4 Star 1 block south of PC
Regina- 4 Star 1 blocks south of PC
Royal Passeig de Gracia- 4 Star 3 blocks west of PC
Royal Ramblas- on the Ramblas
Citadines Ramblas- on the Ramblas
Exe-Ramblas-Boqueria- on the Ramblas
Flor Parks- 4 Star on the Ramblas
Gaudi Ramblas- on the Ramblas
Arc-La Rambla- on the Ramblas
Hotel Monegal- on the Ramblas
Olivia Plaza- 4 Star on the PC
Espana Ramblas- 4 Star on the Ramblas
Gaudi Hotel- 1 block off the Ramblas
Hotel Turin- 1 block off the Ramblas
Oriente Atiram- on the Ramblas
Leonardo Hotel- 3 blocks off the Ramblas
Catalonia Ramblas-4 Star 2 blocks off PC

PC= Plaza Catalonia
All hotels 3 Star unless otherwise noted

APPENDIX B

MADRID HOTELS NEAR ATOCHA

Hotel Mediodia – 2 star across from Atocha
NH Madrid National – 4 star, one block
Hotel Mora by MIJ- 2 star, 3 blocks
Hotel Mexico 2 star, 3 blocks
Radisson Blu Hotel Madrid Prado- 4 star, 4 blocks
Mercure Madrid Centro- 4 star, 5 blocks
CC Atocha- 3 star, 2 blocks
AC Carlton Madrid- 4 star, 2 blocks
NH Madrid Atocha- 3 star, 1 block
Only You Hotel- 4 star, 1 block
AC Hotel Atocha-4 star, 1 block
Hotel Sancho- 3 star, 6 blocks
Rafael Hoteles Atocha- 4 star, 2 blocks
NH Madrid Sur- 3 star, 6 blocks
Catalonia Atocha- 4 star, 5 blocks
Hotel Paseo del Arte (Radisson)- 4 star, 3 blocks
Westin Palace Madrid-5 star, 10 blocks
NH Madrio Paseo- 5 star, 10 blocks
Corbeo -3 star, 10 blocks
One Shot Prado 237 – 3 star 9 blocks
Ibis Stylas -3 star, 10 blocks
Tryp Atochas 4 star, 8 blocks
Vincci Soho 4 star, 10 blocks

Best to confirm walking time from Atocha with hotel.

APPENDIX-C
ENGLISH-SPANISH-CATALAN

ENGLISH	SPANISH	CATALAN
Elevator	ascensor	ascensor
Baggage	equipaje	equipatge
Tickets	billetes	billets
Track	Via	Via Ferria
Money Exchange	Cambio de Moneda	Canui Cie Moneda
Coach	Entrenador de tren	autocar en un tren
Central	Central	Central
Historic area	Zona Historica	Zona Historica
Where is?	Donde esta	On es
Railroad	ferrocarrill	ferrocarrill
Toilette	Aseos/banus	lavabos
ETR fast train	AVE	AVE
Funicular	funicular	funiculor
Grand or large	Grande	gran
Restaurant	restaurante	restaurant

ENGLISH	SPANISH	CATALAN
Arrival	llegada	arribada
Departure Time	Salida	sortida
Plaza	plaza	placa
The Time	La hora	La hora
Help	ayuda	ajudar
Escalator	Escalera mecanica	escalamecanica
Seat	asiento	seient
The check	La quinta	el compte
Thank you	Gracias	gracies
Please	Por fa vor	Si us plau
The Subway	El Metro	El Metro
What time	Que hora es	Que ina hora es
Station	Estation	Estociao

SELECT MAPS

MAP FRONT OF BOOK- ITINERARIES
BARCELONA –RAMBLAS DETAIL
BARCELONA DAY TRIP MONTSERRAT
MADRID CENTRO
MADRID DAY TRIPS- EL ESCORIAL
   AND SEGOVIA
SEGOVIA – CITY DETAILS
MADRID – DAY TRIPS EL ESCORIAL & AVILA
MADRID DAY TRIPS- TOLEDO
CORDOBA – CITY DETAILS
SEVILLE- CITY DETAILS
SEVILLE-CDS DAY TRIPS
   RONDA, GIBRALTAR, TANGIERS
RONDA- CITY DETAILS
MALAGA-MARBELLA
   THE COSTA DEL SOL (CDS)
BILBAO – CITY DETAILS

NOTES-
Not all sites in city are shown
   Most sites are depicted within relationship
     to other sites in the city.
Renfe rail stations shown
Bus stations shown if suggested in chapters

BARCELONA
RAMBLAS DETAIL

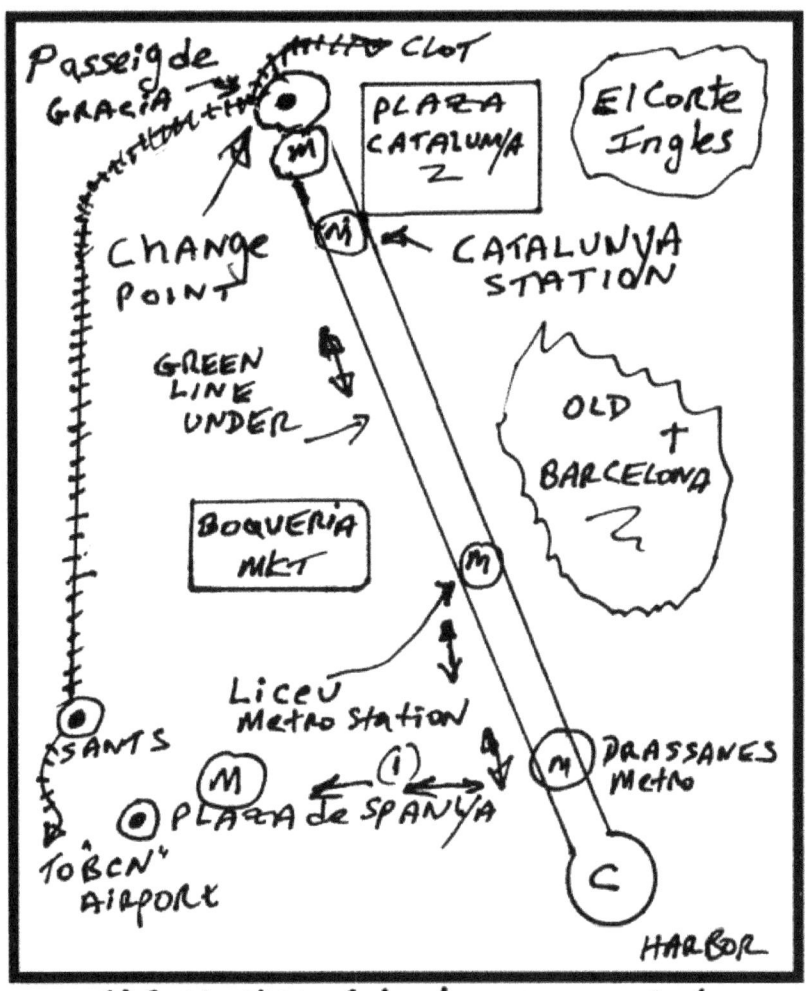

BARCELONA DAY TRIP
MONTSERRAT

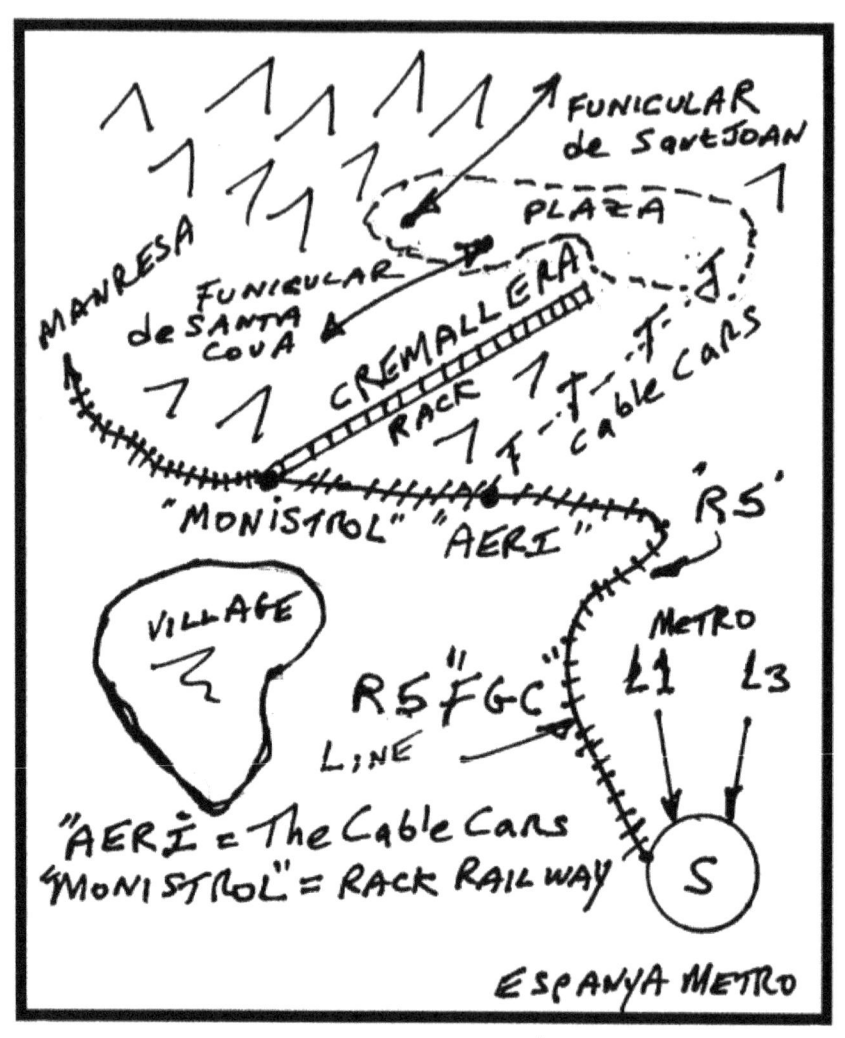

R5 TRAVEL TIME = 60 MINUTES
TOTAL TIME FROM ESPANYA STATION TO "PLAZA" = 90 MINS. ON THE "RACK"

MADRID CENTRO

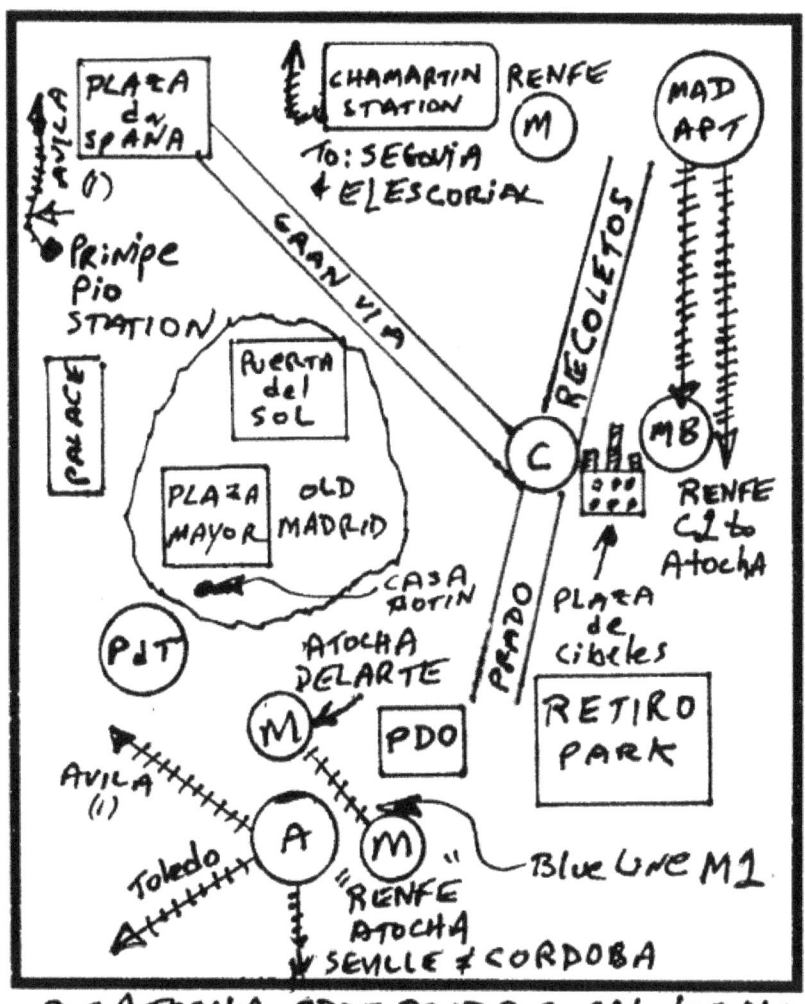

MADRID DAY TRIPS
EL ESCORIAL
AND
SEGOVIA

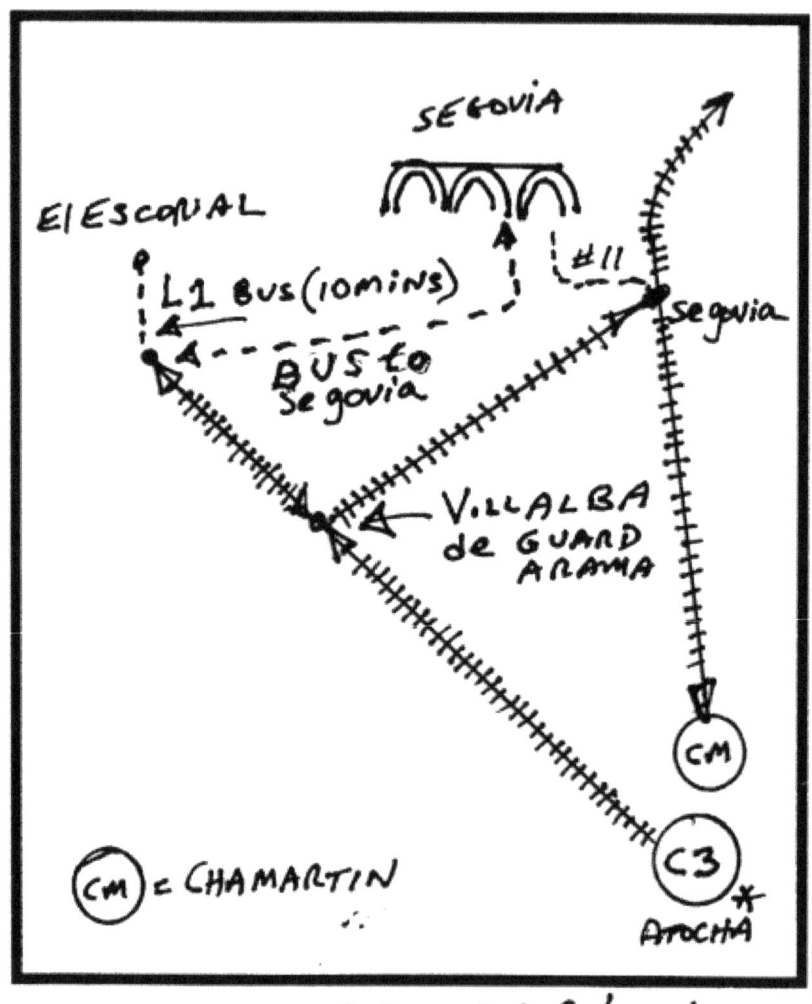

*Also stops at PLAZA de Sol, and others.

SEGOVIA
CITY DETAILS

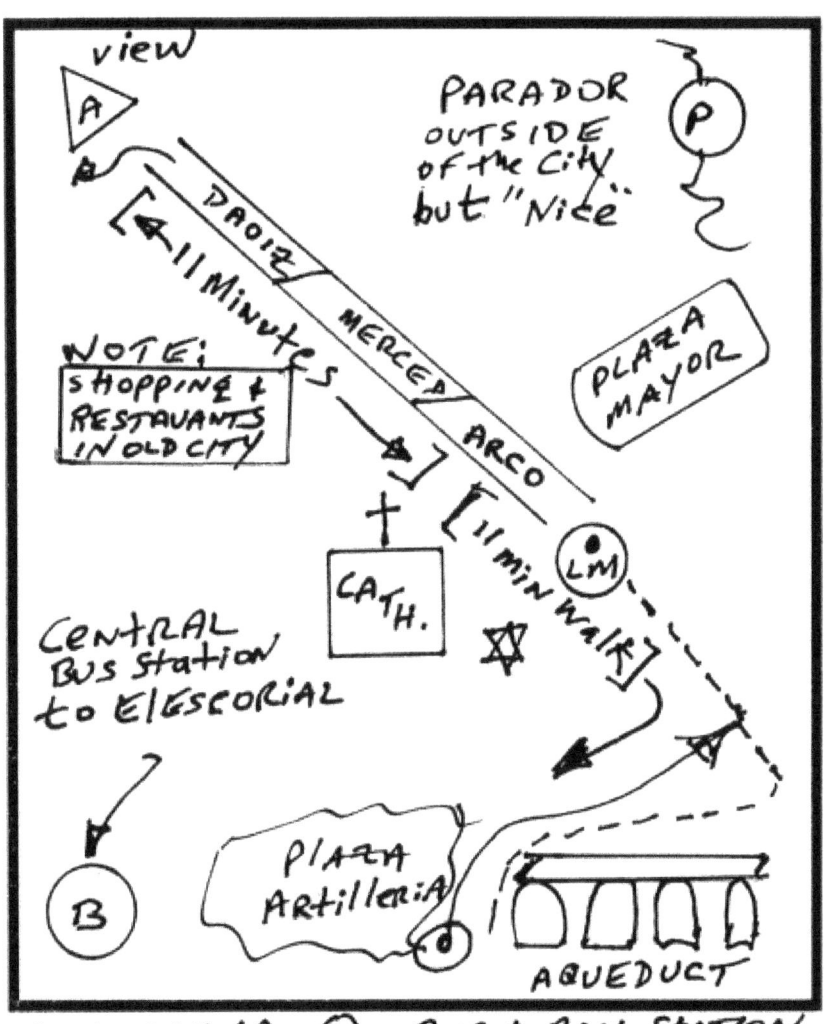

MADRID DAY TRIPS
EL ESCORIAL
AND
AVILA **

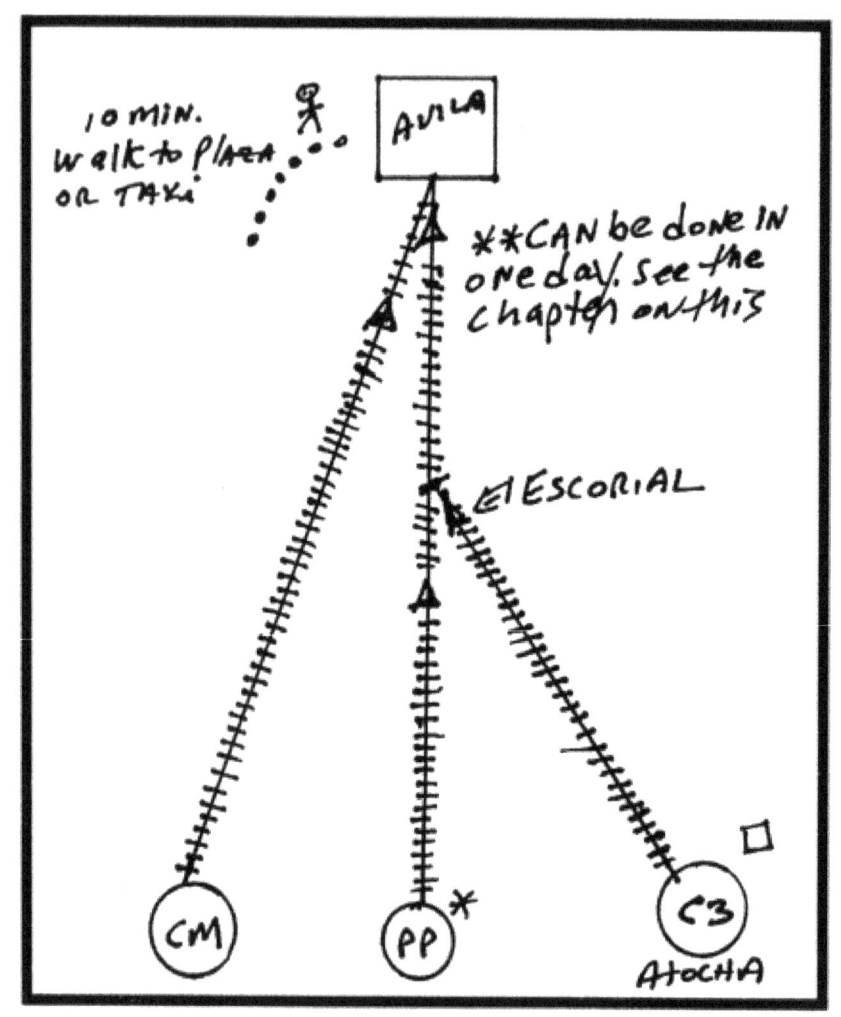

10 MIN. walk to Plaza or Taxi

AVILA

**CAN be done IN one day. see the chapter on this

El ESCORIAL

CM   PP*   C3   ATOCHA

*PP = Most trains to Avila out of "Principe-Pio" station
□ = Note C3 terminates @ Escorial
CM = Chamartin station

MADRID DAY TRIPS
TOLEDO

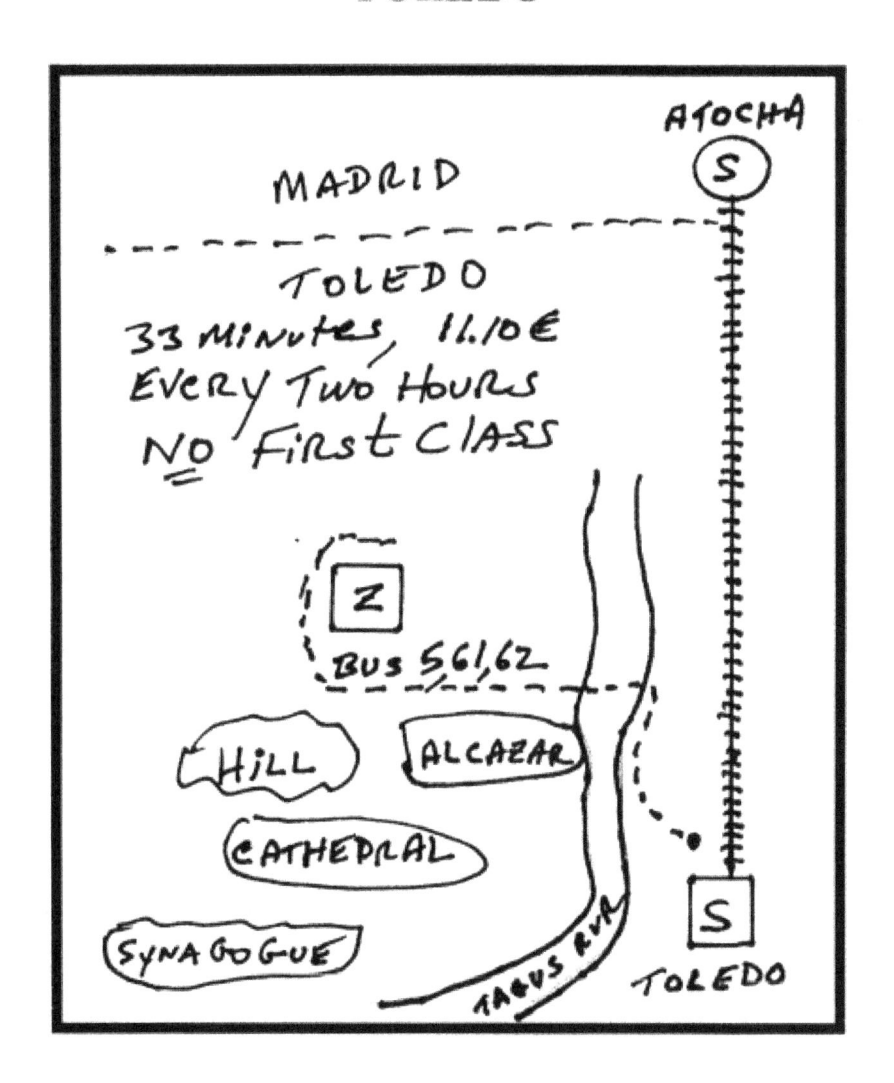

```
                                    ATOCHA
         MADRID                       (S)
    - - - - - - - - - - - - - - -     |
           TOLEDO                     |
       33 MINUTES, 11.10€             |
        EVERY TWO HOURS               |
         NO FIRST CLASS               |
                                      |
              ┌──┐                    |
              │Z │                    |
              └──┘                    |
            BUS 5,61,62               |
                                      |
         ┌────┐  ┌────────┐           |
         │HILL│  │ALCAZAR │           |
         └────┘  └────────┘           |
            ┌──────────┐              |
            │CATHEDRAL │              |
            └──────────┘           ┌─────┐
         ┌──────────┐              │  S  │
         │SYNAGOGUE │              └─────┘
         └──────────┘   TAGUS RVR   TOLEDO
```

Z = Zocodover PLAZA
center of the old walled City
Bus 5 61, & 62 About one Euro
páy on board the bus.

CORDOBA CITY DETAILS

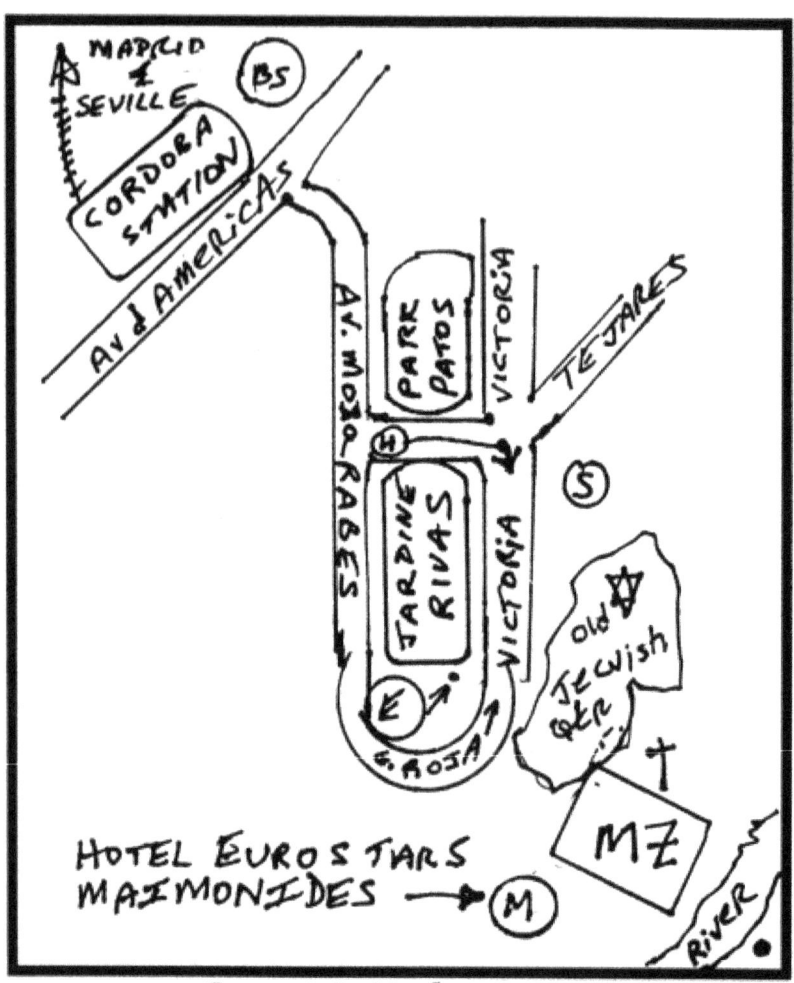

MZ = MEZQUITA E = EUROSTARS HOTEL
(H) = HIROSHIMA/NAGi S = Hotel Selu
BS = BUS STATION ● = Calahorra Tower
and Roman Bridge

SEVILLE
CITY DETAILS

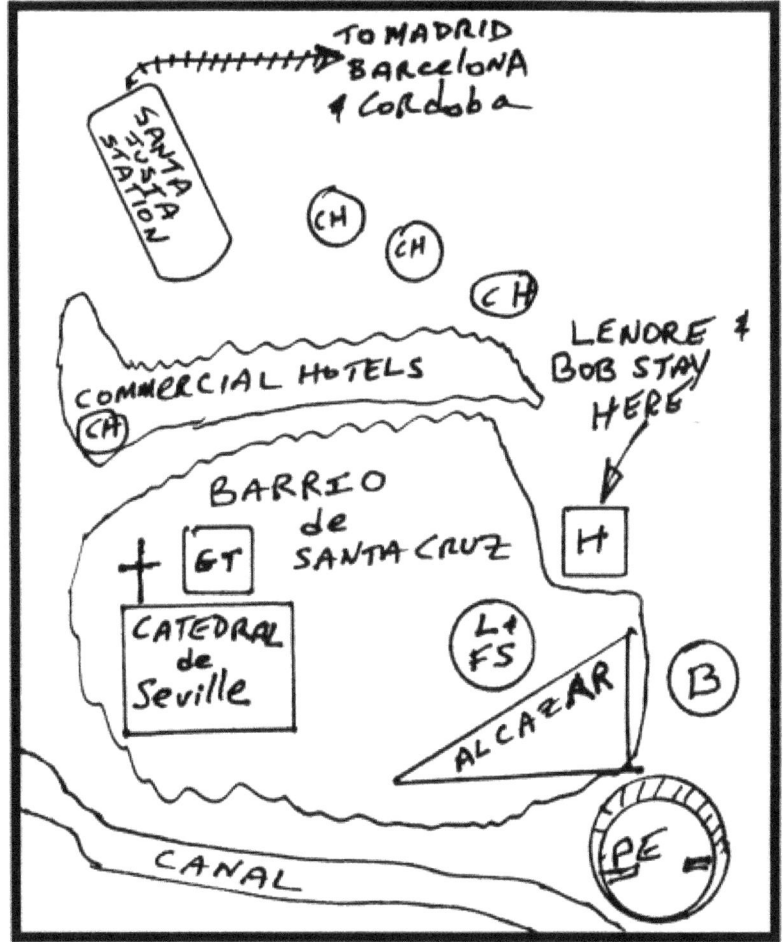

H = Hotel FERNANDO III   B = BUS STATION
GT = GIRALDA TOWER   PE = PLAZA de ESPANYA
L = LA Albahaca & Flamenco Los Gallos
CH = Commercial Hotels

SEVILLE CDS DAY TRIPS
RONDA
GIBRALTAR
TANGIERS

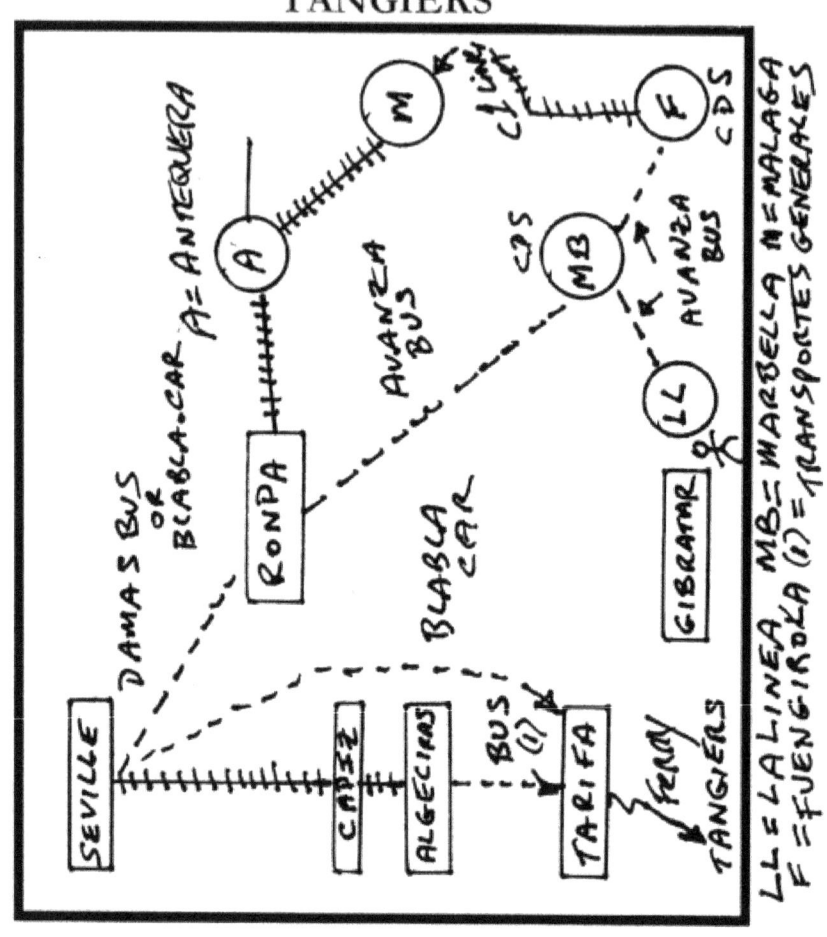

RONDA
CITY DETAILS

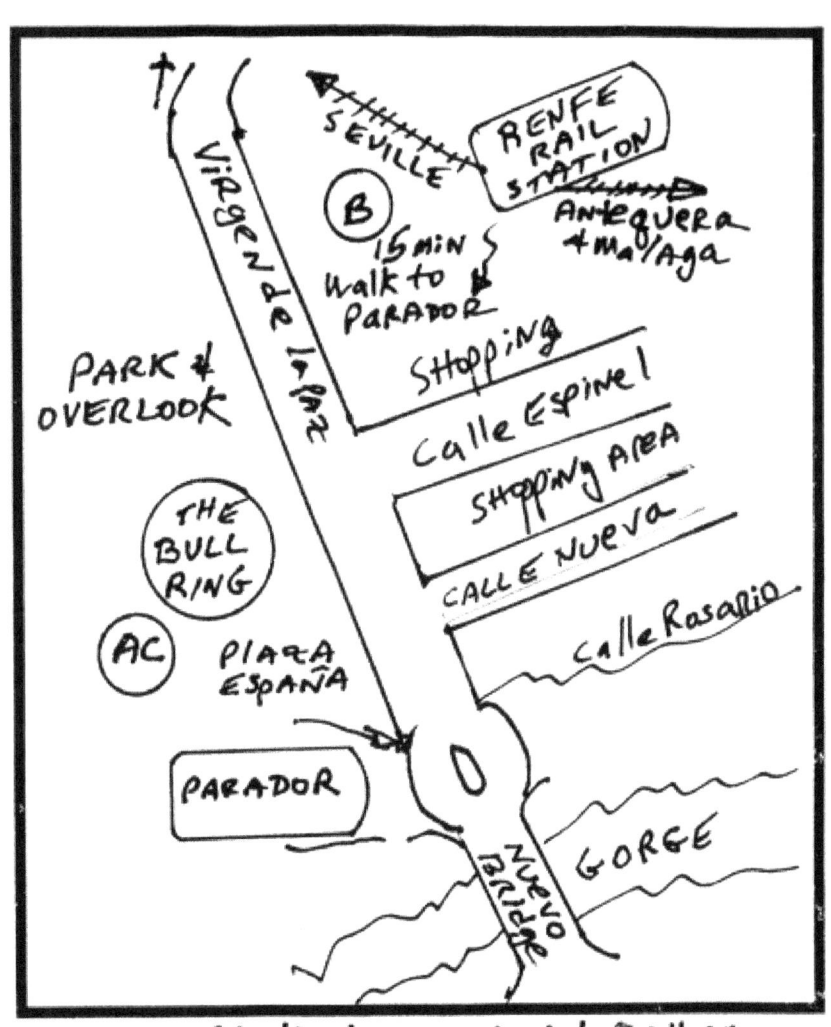

B = BUS STATION AC = ACINIPO HOTEL

MALAGA-MARBELLA
THE COSTA DEL SOL (CDS)

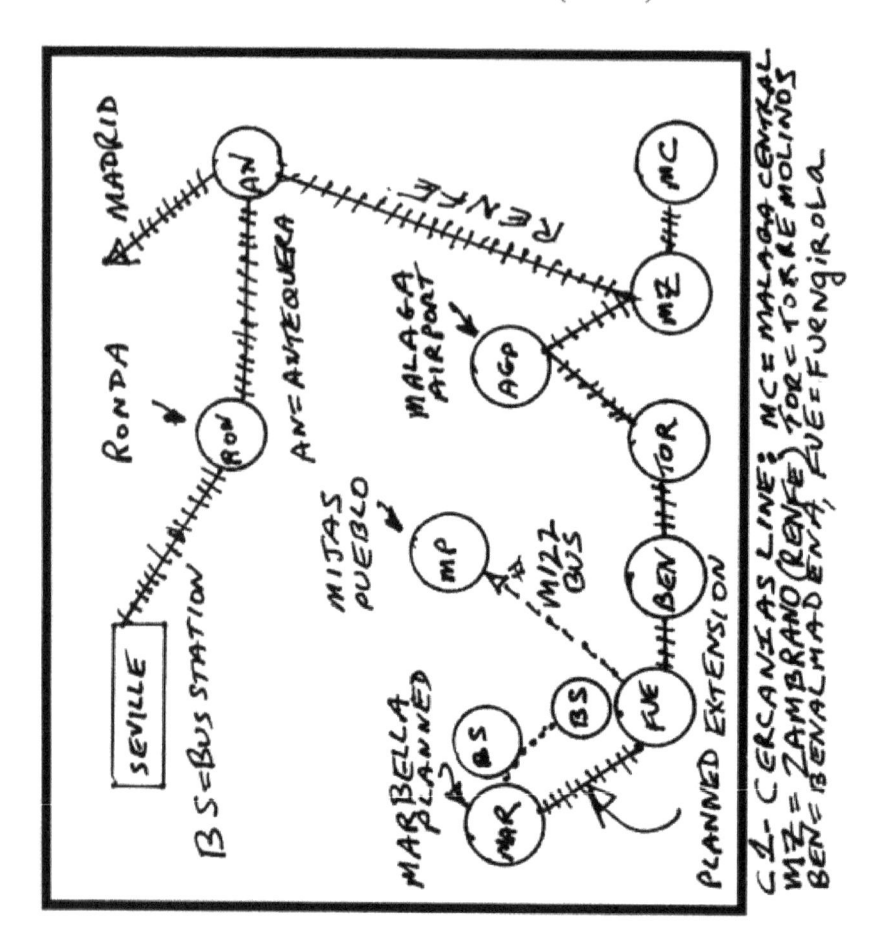

BILBAO- CITY DEAILS

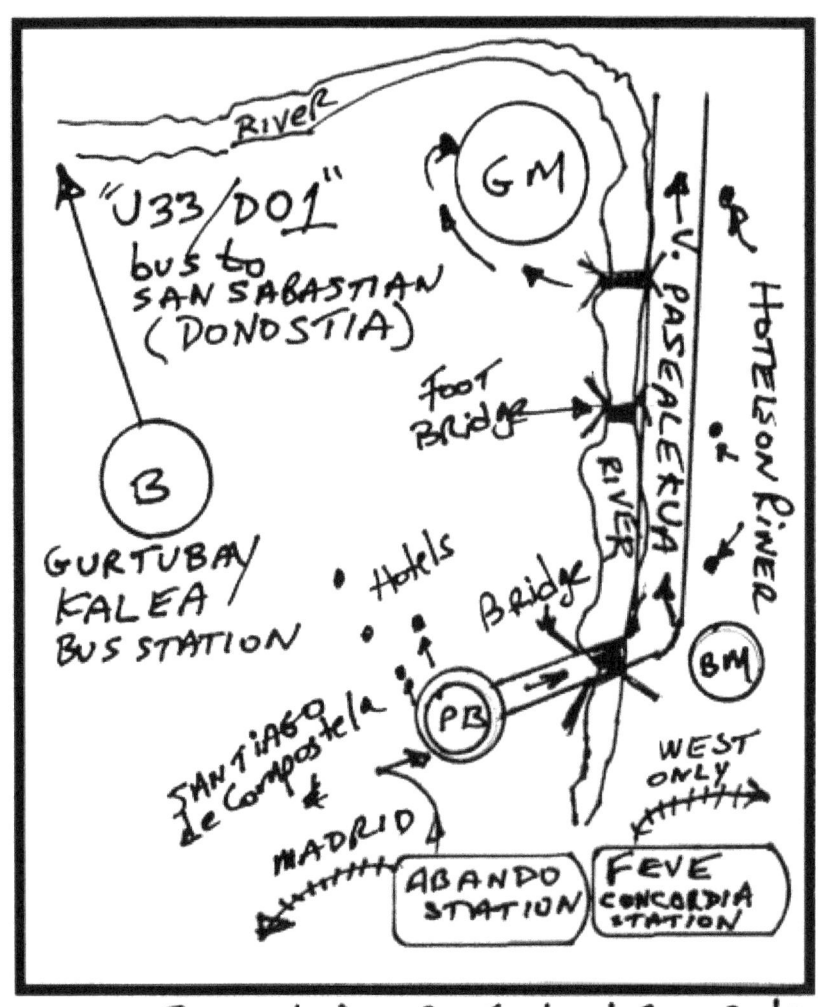

GM = Guggenheim B = Central Bus Stat.
BM = Mega Book MARKET
PB = PLAZA Biribila → walk

Lightning Source UK Ltd.
Milton Keynes UK
UKHW022016060922
408432UK00008B/1788